HOW TO AVOID HOUSEWORK

TIPS, HINTS, AND SECRETS ON HOW TO HAVE A SPOTLESS HOME

PAULA JHUNG

A FIRESIDE BOOK
PUBLISHED BY
SIMON & SCHUSTER
New York London Toronto
Sydney Tokyo Singapore

FIRESIDE
Rockefeller Center
1230 Avenue of the Americas
New York, NY 10020

Copyright © 1995 by Paula Jhung

FIRESIDE and colophon are registered trademarks of
Simon & Schuster Inc.

DESIGNED BY BARBARA MARKS

Manufactured in the United States of America

10 9 8 7 6 5 4 3 2 1

Library of Congress Cataloging-in-Publication Data
Jhung, Paula
    How to avoid housework: tips, hints, and secrets on how to have a spotless
home / Paula Jhung.
        p.   cm.
    "A fireside book."
    Includes index.
    1. House cleaning. 2. Home economics. I. Title.
TX324.J48 1995
648'.5—dc20   95-1953
                      CIP

ISBN 0–684–80267–8

To Larry,

who loves me in spite of it all

Acknowledgments

Thanks to my proofreader and grammarian, Barbara von Rosen. Also to my creative consultants and chief messer-uppers, Kelley and Lisa Jhung. You've given me so much to work with.

CONTENTS

CONFESSIONS
OF A SLOB

My name is Paula, and I'm a slob. I'm lax about putting things away, I'm careless about polishing, and I hate waxing floors.

I'd rather arrange flowers and light candles than dust the table they sit on. I avoid ironing, washing windows, and vacuuming the rug. Yet my house looks pretty decent most of the time. How do I get away with it? I cheat. A lot.

I grew up in a family of eleven: five brothers, two parents, an aunt, an uncle, and a cousin. Because I was the only girl, I had the only single bedroom, a room that was legend throughout the neighborhood. I was either being yelled at or grounded for the piles of clothes on the floor, the unmade bed, and the stuff I could never chuck. But even without the mess the room was ugly. Rickety Victorian pieces darkened its corners; a gray chenille bedspread was meant to cover the bed; and purple, yellow, and gray paper blistered and peeled (with a little help from me) on the walls. I could argue, had I thought of it, that the room was not worth keeping clean, but my mother probably would have swatted me.

Not that she would have earned the Good Housekeeping Seal of Approval. The house was a mess. It wasn't dirty (I never saw a cockroach or a mouse until I had a city apartment of my own), but Mom had no eye for order, and the flotsam and jetsam produced by a household of eleven was staggering. As a survivor of the Depression, she saved

*"You make the beds,
you do the dishes,
and six months later
you have to start all
over again."*
—JOAN RIVERS

every magazine, newspaper, and school paper that came into the house. And there never seemed to be enough money to replace the spring-popped sofa where we kids jumped and wrestled, the chandelier my brother broke practicing his golf swing, or the stain-sucking linoleum my uncle got a deal on. Plus there was a collie who shed year-round and a one-eyed cat who sharpened her claws on the table legs. No wonder my mother was happier tending her garden than dealing with the circus inside.

At sixteen, with money from my first job, I took matters into my own hands. I steamed and stripped the god-awful paper off the walls in my room; replaced the grotesque furniture with some unpainted contemporary pieces I enameled white; painted three of the walls a dusty pink; papered the fourth (very chic at the time) in white, pink, mauve, and gold; and bought a pink quilted comforter shot through with golden threads.

My room looked so good I started my recovery. I knew I'd never be a Suzy Homemaker, but the new look inspired me to keep the room tidier, and it was easier to keep it that way. There was no excess ornamentation in the furniture to trap dust and cobwebs, there was more room to stash my stuff, and the rumpled blankets didn't show nearly as much under the thick comforter. Small discoveries, but I knew I was on to something. I also knew I never wanted to grow up to be one of those TV commercial housewives who fretted over the yellowing of their bathroom bowls, sank into depression with ring around the collar, and constantly worried about waxy buildup.

Still, I struggled to keep my messiness under control. When I went through flight-attendant training, our beds, closets, and drawers were checked every morning; if everything wasn't just so, we'd receive demerits; enough demerits and we were outa there. While everyone else was worried about being sent home for not smiling enough or not passing emergency training, I was scared they were going to find out about the pig in their midst. Somehow they didn't.

Out in the real world, every roommate I ever had was a neatnik by comparison, and I couldn't afford, for financial and psychological reasons, to have them move out in disgust. I read books on getting organized, scoured the closet shops for better ways of dealing with the overflow, and looked for ways to hide the gravy stains from all those TV dinners. But I was inherently lazy, and when company came I would shovel everything into the already bulging closet.

Marriage to Mr. Clean, then having two babies, made avoiding housework more difficult, but I took on the challenge and let adversity propel me forward. Building two houses and remodeling a third gave me the opportunity to find new ways to wage my war against housework. But still I wasn't satisfied. Greed was getting the better of me. What I wanted now was a self-cleaning house.

I went back to school and studied interior design, hoping it would give me further clues and insights into camouflage and decorating secrets. While my younger classmates were swooning over Italian furnishings and French fabrics, I was more interested in low maintenance than in high style. Sure, hand-painted silk pillows are exquisite, but will they hide Ovaltine stains? Will the white Berber survive black track cleats? Will the new down sofa hold up to old bad habits?

I never developed the self-cleaning house, but I did find new ways to deflect the dirt and make it *look* cleaner.

There are thousands of choices to be made when feathering the nest. Choosing well and using a few survival tactics lets us get away with more than we thought we could, and look good, maybe even great, in the process.

Part I

THE NEW
TECHNIQUES

Chapter 1

A NEW
APPROACH

Housework has never been easy, but it was at least manageable when Dad went to work and Mom went to the broom closet.

With Mom out of the closet and in the workforce, the job has become almost overwhelming to men and women alike. Reports show that we spend twenty-six to fifty hours a week on household chores, leaving us with a minimum of free time and energy.

You may have come a long way, baby, but you've got the short end of the broomstick today.

In fact, the farther back we go, the easier it gets. Prehistoric housekeepers had little to do other than sweep the bones out of the cave. Ancient Romans had slaves to keep the bath and vomitorium tidy, and housekeepers in the Dark Ages kept dust and odors in check by throwing a few reeds and herbs around. The average person lived rather simply up until the end of the nineteenth century, when homes started getting cluttered and life became more complicated.

Twentieth-century technology has actually contributed to the glut of household chores. Instead of beating rugs semiannually like Great-grandma, we now feel compelled to vacuum at least weekly. Instead of draping the tables, as was once the practice, we feel pressured to keep them highly polished. Instead of spot-cleaning a few carefully worn garments, we change our clothes sometimes

"Nobody ever died from a little bit of dust."

—HELOISE

THE PERILS OF PERFECTION

They may not be in the medical books, but the following maladies have been known to result from overenthusiastic cleaning and should be avoided at all costs:

- *Carpal tunnel dusting syndrome*
- *Polishing elbow*
- *Carpet cleaner's cramps*
- *TBCS, or toilet-bowl-cleaner sensitivity*
- *Mopping migraine*
- *Floor scrubber's water-on-the-knee*
- *Vacuum hearing loss*
- *Dustpan depression*
- *Window washer's bursitis*
- *Sweeper's shoulder*

"Housework can kill you if you do it right."

—ERMA BOMBECK

two or three times a day, then face mountains of wash every week.

Technology has given us high-speed buffers so we can have glossy floors, state-of-the-art fabric finishes so we can upholster in white wool and pale silk, and sophisticated kitchen equipment so we can dine in gourmet elegance. Sure we can.

Why do we set such unrealistic standards for ourselves when our lives are already so complicated?

We've been conditioned. Before we could walk, we were read stories about the virtues of housework. Beauty kept out of trouble with chores before she met Beast, Cinderella developed an appealing modesty by scrubbing, and Snow White stayed safe by sweeping up after seven little men.

TV is also a factor. You'd think June Cleaver was still dusting lightbulbs by the looks of things. But no, Mom's either performing brain surgery, reporting world events, or defending civil rights. Attorney Clair Huxtable has a large family, who, along with their friends, raid the fridge, watch

TV, and dance in the living room. Yet despite the absence of a maid, there are never crumbs on the counter, sweatshirts on the sofa, or homework piled on the dining table. Murphy Brown's apartment is still as clean and orderly as it was before she had the kid. And you never see anyone actually wash those satin sheets or *make* those designer beds they're so quick to jump into on the soaps.

Decorating magazines also perpetrate the spotless-house myth. There are never newspapers, magazines, or mail strewn about, no bulging closets, no dirty dishes in the sink. Comparing our less-than-perfect surroundings with those in *House Beautiful* is like comparing our less-than-perfect bodies with those we see in *Vogue*. Maybe if we starve ourselves and work out like maniacs every day we'll start to resemble high-fashion models, and maybe if we chain ourselves to the vacuum cleaner and pin dust mitts to our sleeves we'll have model-clean homes. But do we want "homeorexia" as well as the anorexia that may result from setting such unrealistic standards?

In his book, *Home, a Short History of an Idea*, architecture professor Witold Rybczynski writes:

> Hominess is not neatness. Otherwise everyone would live in replicas of the kinds of sterile and impersonal homes that appear in interior design and architectural magazines. What these spotless rooms lack, or what crafty photographers have carefully removed, is any evidence of human occupation. In spite of the artfully placed vases and casually arranged art books, the imprint of their inhabitants is missing. These pristine interiors fascinate and repel me. Can people really live without clutter? How do they stop the Sunday papers from spreading all over the living room? How do they manage without toothpaste tubes and half-used soap bars in their bathrooms? Where do they hide the detritus of their everyday lives?

"A house unkempt cannot be so distressing as a life unlived."
—ROSE MACAULAY

*"Homes are built to
live in, more than to
look on."*

—FRANCIS BACON

There are those who "hide the detritus of their . . . lives" quite well. We all know the fanatically house-proud person who maintains a museum of a home, a home that seems to have a velvet rope across each room, where family members tiptoe around for fear of making it look like someone actually lived there.

Few of us feel comfortable in these monuments to housekeeping one psychologist describes as "places where the furnishings flourish, but the spirit surely wilts."

We're afraid we'll upset the balance of nature by putting down a teacup next to the carefully arranged tablescape or actually reading one of those coffee-table books. Whether it's the overly calculated decor, or the fuss-budget attitude of the keeper, most of us want out.

I had a next-door neighbor whose apartment was far from a paragon of order. It seemed permanently littered with books, projects, and other paraphernalia. There was always a game or puzzle set up somewhere, and the coffeepot was always on. It was set up more to accommodate her friends than to impress them—the kind of place you could drop by, plop down, and feel perfectly at home. I mourned when she moved and hope she never discovered domestic perfection.

Yet we all crave order and beauty. "People are doing less housework because they don't have the time," observes household tips expert Mary Ellen Pinkham, "but they're very concerned about how their homes look."

The home should provide refuge from this crazy world instead of making us crazy trying to keep it. Keeping sane while keeping house means replacing the pursuit of perfection for a more realistic approach: like chucking that stain-prone rug, putting away the doodads that always need dusting, and simply closing the door on that landfill your kid calls a bedroom.

We can also eliminate the tedious and the time consuming through the use of dirt-deflecting materials; easy-to-maintain furnishings; and the art of illusion, camouflage, and delegation.

It *is* possible to have reasonably clean and orderly surroundings without knocking ourselves for a loop. We just need to lighten up, pare down, and take a new approach to this age-old problem.

"The height of security is not to give a damn."

—MARIO BUATTA

Chapter 2

An Ounce
of Prevention

"Housework can't kill you, but why take the risk?"

—Phyllis Diller

Listen. Can you hear it? It's the sound of dust, dander, and dirt drifting, scratching, and marching into our homes, mucking up our floors, soiling our fabrics, and adding hours to our workweek. If we can keep them at bay, we can get a leg up on housework.

Park Those Pumas

The Carpet and Rug Institute estimates 80 percent of the dirt in our homes hitchhikes in on our shoes. Considering the wafflelike soles most of us wear and the muck they wade through in the course of a day, it's easy to see why.

Doormats help, but they're not the answer. At least not with the deeply embedded soles of the athletic shoes that are so popular today. Besides, few people actually shuffle before entering, and simply walking across even the best-designed mat won't pull the dirt out of those Michelin-like treads. Mats even add to the problem by becoming saturated with dirt and drifting it, along with worn bits of fiber, plastic, or rubber, inside.

Inside mats carry the added hassle of having to move them every time we vacuum, sweep, or mop. They also detract from the decor and, when we don't clean them often enough, just add to the household dirt.

Great Britain's National Trust, an organization that

preserves, maintains, and shows historic properties, has found at least three feet of absorbent matting is needed to clean flat-soled shoes. But there doesn't seem to be enough matting in the United Kingdom to handle the deeply embossed soles favored by tourists. The dirt they deposit has been so damaging to the Trust's manor houses, palaces, and castles, they're experimenting with other preventive measures, including vinyl or paper slippers to be worn over shoes, especially in inclement weather.

"Housekeeping ain't no joke."
—LOUISA MAY ALCOTT

Paper slippers were the answer to a prayer for the Mormon Church when it opened its new temple in San Diego in the spring of '93. The thousands of visitors who tramped through its hallowed halls were issued disposable shoe covers to protect the new carpeting and marble floors from a holy mess of mud, grit, and germs.

Booties are also issued to tourists at Hawaii's Iolani Palace to protect the century-old Douglas fir floors from the ravages of sandy soles.

In our own homes, the best way to avoid tread dirt is to get in the habit of trading "outside shoes" for "inside shoes," slippers, or socks at the door. It may seem like a hassle at first, but it becomes habit over time.

The Korean side of our family made a believer out of me. It took a while to catch on, but I finally realized why their floors looked better than mine, with half the hassle. By removing their shoes, they leave the dirt that grimes up the house outside, where it belongs. From Tokyo to Istanbul, half the world leaves its shoes at the door, and half the world's floors stay clean without the benefit of electric cleaners, shampooers, and buffers. It's time we got with it.

• Set up a bench or chair by the family entrance for easy shoe removal.

• Buy or build a low cabinet or bookcase to house shoes and slippers.

• Keep "room shoes" (shoes that never leave the house), slippers, or socks on a shelf or in a large basket or bin.

• Ask workers to remove their shoes, and hope

"There are two types of dirt: the dark kind, attracted to light objects; and the light kind, attracted to dark objects."

—ELY SLICK

guests will. But don't worry too much about outsiders. Ninety percent of dirt is generated by the household.

• Keep a boot brush outside the door to dislodge clumps of dirt before boots are brought into the "shoe room."

• Be especially vigilant in winter. The salts and other chemicals used to melt ice and snow are tracked in and break down fibers and finishes.

SHUN SCUM, SPOTS, AND SCALE

Hard water means hard work—in the form of spotted dishes, gray laundry, crusty showerheads, and ring around the tub and toilet bowl.

Well water can be nasty too, since its high iron content leaves rust stains on clothes, around drains, and anywhere else it touches. Iron also corrodes pipes, water heaters, and ice makers.

A water-softening unit removes these problem minerals by filtering them through tiny resin beads coated with sodium ions. The softened water then flows through the faucets, and the mineral brine that causes scum, spots, and residue is flushed away.

In addition to reducing housework, softened water also prolongs the life of water-using appliances, increases

SICK OF DIRT

Shoe removal not only adds to the life of floors but may add to our own longevity as well. In a test house at the Southwest Research Institute in San Antonio, scientists found sixteen different toxins, including pesticides and lead dust, had been tracked in on the soles of shoes. Pesticides can remain active for years and lead dust attacks the nervous system. Children are at highest risk with their developing bodies and proximity to the floor; babies crawl and taste everything they see there, including the carpet, and older children spend much of their time there, playing, reading, and watching TV.

A DAY IN THE LIFE OF A SHOE

7:00 A.M. *Out of the closet onto the feet.*

7:45 A.M. *Down the subway stairs wading through sticky papers, wads of gum, and puddles of stale beer.*

8:15 A.M. *Into the workplace with hundreds of other soles. Who knows where they've been?*

10:00 A.M. *Rest-room break. Floors are a little wet around the toilet. Hmmmm.*

12:00 P.M. *Lunch in the park. Watch out for the dog poop!*

5:30 P.M. *The market. Nice and clean here. I hear they spray the floors regularly to keep roaches under control.*

6:00 P.M. *Home again. Must inspect the lawn to see if the herbicide is doing the job on the weeds.*

6:10 P.M. *Think I'll just rest up here on the coffee table awhile. Wonder why the new carpet looks so grungy? The dog doesn't look so good either. That woman is scrubbing again. Says those damn floors are going to be the death of her yet.*

the efficiency of water heaters, and, since it dissolves scale, boosts the water flow in pipes.

Except for the salt you have to feed it every so often, a water softener requires little maintenance. However, it does consume water—about a shower's worth weekly to flush out contaminants.

Unit prices vary widely. Water-softening companies generally charge more, appliance stores and home centers less.

• Use potassium granules instead of salt if you're on a septic system. Salt destroys the bacteria that break down solids in a septic system.

• If you're hooked up to a municipal sewer system, check to see if your community allows water softeners. Some cities have banned new installations because of water-reclamation projects.

• Install a backflow preventer to keep sewer water

from touching the drainpipe. "Mr. Drain" is the trade name of one such device.

• Buy a water-softening unit with a wide opening to make salt or potassium refills easy.

• Choose a demand-control unit, one that regenerates according to fluctuating water use, rather than a timed model that generates automatically whether it needs it or not. A demand-control unit uses less water.

• If there's a high iron content in the water supply, install an oxidizing filtering system in place of, or in addition to, a conventional unit.

• Avoid having a water-softening company test for hardness. It's like asking a car dealer if you need another car. Instead, buy a water-testing kit from a hardware store or home center, or have water tested by a state-certified agency or private lab. Check the Yellow Pages under "Laboratories Testing."

• Don't expect a water softener to make water more palatable. It removes work-making minerals, not unpleasant odor and taste.

• If a water softener isn't in the picture for you, use Borax or a water-conditioning powder like White King in the washing machine, Calgon in the tub, and a cup or so of white vinegar in the dishwasher.

DEFY DUST

An air purifier may be one of the best-kept secrets when it comes to dodging the dust rag. Museums, art galleries, and fine antique shops have long used them to reduce maintenance and protect their merchandise. Allergy sufferers who use them find their sinuses as well as their homes stay cleaner. They're also useful if there's a smoker in the house, for the health of the nonsmokers as well as for the appearance and life span of fabrics and finishes.

Purifiers use various types of filtration to trap or suck out airborne dust. Some are simple pleated fiber panels that fit the return duct of the central furnace and air

THE AGE-OLD QUEST FOR BETTER WATER

People have been struggling to clean up their water supplies since the beginning of civilization. Ancient Egyptians siphoned water out of clay drums, leaving sediment behind. Sparta's water was so foul a cup was designed to disguise its unappetizing color and gunk. Romans built miles of aqueducts to transport pure mountain water into their cities. Unfortunately, the aqueducts were lined with lead, now known to be toxic.

In Renaissance Venice, rainwater was filtered through earth and sand much like modern municipal systems that use layers of anthracite coal and sand to remove suspended solids.

Today, distillation, carbon filters, and reverse-osmosis devices further purify drinking water, and water softeners remove the mineral crud that complicates housework.

conditioner. They retail for under ten dollars and are fairly effective if they're changed semiannually. Others, like electronic furnace panels and portable floor units, are more sophisticated, expensive, and proficient.

• In order for an air cleaner to be effective, make sure windows and doors are weather sealed and all cracks and crevices are plugged.

• Count on an air cleaner to zap airborne dust before it lands, not to clean an already dusty room.

• Replace disposable furnace and central air-conditioning filters at the beginning or end of each heating and cooling season.

• Keep the furnace fan on even when the heat is off.

• Toss electronic filters in the dishwasher twice a year.

• Expect a floor unit to bust dust only in the room it's in.

• Expect little from a tabletop unit. Because of its compact size, it's unable to process much air.

• Have the air ducts professionally cleaned. They're tough to reach with their twists and turns and often have such an accumulation of oil, dust, and dirt, it gets blown through the house.

CONFINE DINING

When every room is a dining room, every surface is fair game for crumbs, splatters, and stains. Do yourself a favor, and confine meals and snacks to the easily maintained spaces they were designed for.

RESTRICT ROVER

One of the easiest ways to avoid hard-core cleaning is to avoid having furry friends. But since they're sometimes preferable to the human kind, taking a few preventive measures helps us keep Rover and Kitty as well as our sanity. Housing them outside, or at least keeping them restricted to certain areas inside, cuts down on scratched table legs, carpet stains, and hairy upholstery.

- Keep the home fairly free from fur of indoor/outdoor pets by stapling strips of Velcro around the pet door.
- Restrict the dog to the kitchen to keep the rest of the house flea, fur, and dander free, and to ensure the floor gets a regular tongue scrubbing.

YOU NEED PREVENTATIVE MEASURES WHEN

- *Your floors look like a fertilizer farm and need to be swept or vacuumed every time you turn around.*
- *The furnishings are so dusty they'd look at home in the Addams family mansion.*
- *Your sofa is colored and patterned with salsa stains, cola spills, and crushed cookie crumbs.*
- *Your once-clear drinking glasses have frosted.*
- *That formerly snow-white warm-up has turned grungy gray.*
- *There are mysterious orange spots on your favorite white jeans.*
- *That comfy velvet chair looks like it's been slipcovered in kitty-colored fur.*
- *The family thinks the dining room is anywhere in front of the TV.*

Chapter 3

THE NEW MIX

Our decorating style pretty much determines just how much time and energy we need to keep the place up.

Generally speaking, an informal, relaxed look is a lot easier to maintain than a formal style that needs constant spit and polish. But every style has its maintenance strengths and weaknesses. By knowing what they are we can adopt and adapt anything from early cave to postmodern.

"With a good mix you don't have the stale kind of model home look that's matchey-match and here today and gone tomorrow," said Wendy Livesay Grumet, an award-winning interior designer. "What you'll have is a look of timelessness."

With timelessness and timesaving in mind, some of the vices and virtues of today's most popular decorating styles are listed below.

> *"Use what works.*
> *If Louis XIV had had*
> *it, he would have*
> *used Formica and*
> *track lighting."*
> —INTERIOR DESIGNER
> EDWARD ZAJAC

AMERICAN COUNTRY

Homey, casual, and comfortable, American Country is the kind of look you can prop your feet up on. Scratches, dents, and peeling paint add to the character of the already well-worn woods; and old chests, Shaker boxes, and decorative pegs combine storage with style.

Plus, warm muted prints of cranberry, camel, and gold camouflage peanut-butter-and-jelly stains; while natural fabrics like gingham, chintz, and calico easily come clean in the wash.

The problem with country is that it feeds the fantasies of the collector. Too much stuff can turn it into a cleaning nightmare. Restraint pays off here.

The advantages:
- the "plain and simple" Shaker philosophy
- handcrafted irregularity
- heavily grained woods like knotty pine, oak, and maple
- multipurpose furnishings like storage benches and coffee table/chests
- large cupboards that store dust catchers
- sponge-painted furniture
- low-gloss finishes
- bare wood floors
- cafe curtains
- ironware
- small dense prints
- deep rich plaids
- afghans and patchwork quilts
- durable denims
- pewter and tin
- stenciling

The disadvantages:
- dust-catching dried floral arrangements
- difficult-to-clean twig furniture
- an abundance of floor cloths
- too many "things"

CONTEMPORARY

Spare, sleek, and understated, this is a look that gives maximum effect with a minimum of furnishings. Never fussy, it has clean lines and smooth surfaces that make it one of the easiest styles to maintain.

Easy-care elements are:
- flecked, low-napped, commercial or Berber carpeting
- bare floors
- machine-washable cotton dhurrie rugs
- stainless steel
- recessed lighting
- vertical blinds and simple crisp shades
- Scandinavian-designed, highly functional furnishings
- whitewashed and light-toned woods with urethane finishes
- plastic laminate and polyester cabinets
- built-in storage
- large-scale furnishings (fewer pieces to maintain)
- tile and stone flooring
- highly textured fabrics that create a soil-disguising light/shadow effect

While smooth, glossy surfaces usually mean smooth cleaning, care should be taken with contemporary trademark materials and colors: mirror, lacquer, and chrome show every fingerprint, and clear, pale colors, as well as stark white and solid black showcase soil and dust. Better to go with low-gloss surfaces, contrasting textures, and rich jewel tones, or warm, earthy neutrals.

In its pure form, contemporary can be as cold and impersonal as a motel lobby. More than any other style, it benefits from a mix with older and warmer furnishings.

SOUTHWEST

A blend of Mexican, Native American, and Anglo influences, this earthy yet sophisticated style is a natural in many settings.

Rugged pine furnishings take on a patina with wear, and geometric Native American prints hide soil till you're ready to deal with it.

The advantages:
- mission-style furnishings
- equipales: handmade Mexican pigskin and wood chairs
- warm earth tones
- bleached, weathered, and distressed (artfully marred) woods
- Navajo rugs and blankets
- animal prints
- serape cloth
- Guatemalan textiles
- buffalo-plaid blankets
- terra-cotta pottery
- Mexican tile floors
- painted wood furniture
- turquoise and tin accessories
- a broken-in, handcrafted look
- natural, soil-releasing fabrics
- "bancos"—plastered, built-in seating-storage/room dividers

The disadvantages:
- white Haitian cotton that absorbs soil like a sponge
- sisal rugs that fray
- silver accessories that tarnish
- too many wooden coyotes, snakes, and jackrabbits—overdone and overdusted

COUNTRY FRENCH

A kissing cousin of American Country, the Gallic look has provincial warmth, but its heavily carved surfaces and reliance on clutter make it a challenge to keep clean.

The advantages:
- richly colored, soil-hiding miniprints
- pickled woods
- faux-rusted wrought iron
- distressed pine
- earthenware bowls

NEAT TRICKS

1. Protect a good sofa, or conceal one that's seen better days, with a colorful afghan or patchwork quilt.

2. Apply a crackle finish to a new table for instant aging and a forgiving surface. Crackle kits are easy to use and are available at hobby and craft stores.

3. Choose glass over a Plexiglas coffee table. Plexiglas scratches easily and is permanently clouded by alcohol, lemonade, and even glass cleaners.

4. Give an object space. An inexpensive vase can look like a treasure if it is not lost in a sea of accessories. Savor it, or store it.

5. Instead of sun-bleached pastels, decorate with soil-hiding colors of soft sage, dusty blue, and smoky lavender.

6. Buy a tree-sized cactus to add a fresh, sculptural quality to a room. Its only requirements are decent light and a tall drink every so often.

7. Invest in a stone-topped coffee table. Stone takes lots of abuse, shows little dust, and needs no polishing.

8. Hunt down an old farm table for the kitchen. It will provide a rugged, easy-care surface on which to do homework, mix up a batch of biscuits, or dine.

9. Buy a French baker's rack to mass houseplants for effect, humidity, and easy watering.

10. A butler's tray on a sturdy base makes a handsome and practical coffee table. Instead of individually gathering cups or glasses at the end of an evening, simply lift the whole table top and ferry its contents to the kitchen.

11. Choose an elegantly simple Williamsburg chandelier in pewter or brass instead of a crystal fixture dripping with prisms and eventually cobwebs and dust.

12. Queen Anne dining chairs usually have seat cushions that are easily removed. Stretch and staple densely printed fabric over the old, and pop the cushion back into the frame.

13. Wainscoting, a different treatment on the lower third of a wall, has long been a popular look in period settings. Cover the lower wall in a densely printed canvas-backed vinyl, and top with chair-rail molding to camouflage fingerprints from the four-foot-and-under crowd.

14. Cover side tables with pretty, floor-length skirts and glass rounds and you'll never have to wax and polish them again.

- terra-cotta tile floors
- hand-painted tiles
- used brick walls (except in the kitchen)
- armoires that hide sound and video equipment, linens, or bar supplies
- verdigris finishes

The disadvantages:
- heavy carving
- linen, ribbons, and lace
- hanging brass and copper pots in the kitchen (grease catchers that need frequent polishing)
- antique bed linens

BLENDING IT BEAUTIFULLY

The most successful blends of furnishings have unifying threads that pull unrelated items together. To transform a patchwork of odds and ends into your own unique tapestry:
- *Use one tone liberally throughout the room. Color is the great unifier.*
- *Consider the following guideline for using color:*

  60 percent   floors and walls, closely related tones
  30 percent   upholstery and draperies, harmonizing tones
  10 percent   accessories, contrasting tones
- *Repeat room colors in the garden beyond.*
- *Use restraint with patterns. A mix of understated prints is more cohesive than bold, "look at me" designs.*
- *Use geometrics to pull it together. A crisp stripe, dot, or grid on walls or furnishings seems to bring order out of chaos.*
- *Keep wall and window treatments elegantly simple.*
- *Create pleasing spatial relationships by placing lamp shades at about the same height and lining up the tops or bottoms of picture frames.*
- *Keep furnishings in scale. A large easy chair needs a large ottoman or stool. A small, delicate desk calls for a small, graceful lamp.*
- *Under- rather than overfurnish. A successful mix has plenty of breathing room.*

EIGHTEENTH-CENTURY ENGLISH

Formal, symmetrical, and tailored, this is one of the more challenging styles to maintain. What it has going for it is its elegant simplicity.

The advantages:
- glazed cottons
- tapestry prints
- dense florals
- rich paisleys
- intricately patterned Persian rugs
- pewter accessories
- tilt-top and drop-leaf tables that save space and add flexibility

The disadvantages:
- glossy, flawless woods
- fluted, scalloped, and carved ornamentation
- fragile damasks, silks, and brocades
- china figurines
- crystal chandeliers
- silver accessories
- overly ornate picture frames
- draperies that "puddle" to the floor
- tassels, tufting, and trim

VICTORIAN

A romantic look, but with its emphasis on collectibles, and layer upon layer of fabric, this style is tough to maintain.

The advantages:
- large-scaled floral prints, paisleys, and tapestries
- glazed cottons
- cut and crushed velvet
- multicolored carpeting in tight geometric or floral prints

"Imagination is more important than knowledge."
—ALBERT EINSTEIN

"There is nothing duller than perfectly good taste."
—BILLY BALDWIN

"Elegance is the art of not astonishing."
—JEAN COCTEAU

THE MOST POPULAR STYLES

According to a 1994 Family Circle *survey, the following styles were most favored by readers:*

1. *American country, 26 percent*
2. *Contemporary, 19 percent*
3. *Eclectic, 10 percent*
4. *Formal/traditional, 9 percent*
5. *Country cottage, 7 percent*
     Comfort was the most important factor respondents said they sought when redecorating their homes.

"Nobody is buying Chippendale anymore. It's too expensive and too fussy. People don't want to dust it."
—TERRY KOVEL, *KOVELS' ANTIQUES AND COLLECTIBLES PRICE LIST*

"Style is a search for greater freedom. You don't need money or culture, just a bit of courage and a lot of passion."
—FRENCH DESIGNER STEPHAN JANSON

- deep, muted colors
- crazy quilts
- decorative screens that hide clutter

The disadvantages:

- intricately carved, dark and glossy woods
- tufted upholstery
- brass beds
- elaborate window treatments
- starched lace, damask, smooth velvets, moiré taffeta
- ornately framed and beribboned mirrors and pictures
- bric-a-brac, memorabilia
- beadwork, tassels, buttons, and fringe

Chapter 4

THE FINE ART
OF DELEGATION

The dream is to have the family so well trained you hardly have to lift a finger. The reality is they think helping out means lifting their legs as you vacuum around the sofa.

Those couch potatoes need to shoulder more of the load, though asking them to "help" may be the wrong approach.

Family therapist Dr. Nora La Corte believes the word "help" implies the wife and mother is the primary housekeeper regardless of whether or not she works outside the home.

"When a woman asks, 'Will you help with my work?' The response often is 'I've got my own work to do,'" said La Corte.

She believes if the whole family shares the home, the whole family should care for it. "When a woman is mainly responsible for the home, she's worn to the point of exhaustion. If she doesn't build a team mentality, hostility sets in.

"We need to think of ourselves as 'home managers,' " she said. "If you're a manager, you have a team. A team that has a sense of empowerment and works for the commonweal of the family."

"When men do the dishes, it's called helping. When women do the dishes, it is called life."
—ANNA QUINDLEN, NEW YORK TIMES

SELLING YOUR SPOUSE

The first player to recruit to the team is your partner. When the children see that Mom and Dad share the load, they're more willing to be part of the action.

• Verbalize. Many of us are socialized to beat around the bush when it comes to our own needs. We hope others will pick up on what we think is the obvious, and we're hurt when they don't. Nuances don't work. Clarity does.

• Choose the time and place well for a heart-to-heart talk on the benefits of partnership. A candlelit restaurant on a Saturday night is good. Monday morning when all hell is breaking loose is not.

• Be specific. Instead of saying you need more help, identify exactly what needs to be done.

• Appeal to your mutual love and respect as well as his strength, energy, and any other qualities you can tap into.

• Point out the perks. There's not only a happier you, there's a healthier him. According to a University of Washington study, husbands who share the household chores with their wives are emotionally and physically healthier than those who don't.

USING PSYCHOLOGY

• Flatter. "The baby seems so much happier when you bathe him." "I wish I could organize a closet as well as you." "How do you get that floor looking so good?"

• Lavish praise. We all respond better to positive reinforcement than we do to criticism.

• Reject ownership. Never call appliances, rooms, or cleaning equipment "mine." They are always "ours." When you give up ownership of something, you give up the sole responsibility of operating or maintaining it.

• Back off. The more you do, the less your partner will do.

TRAINING

- Spell out exactly what a job entails. To you, cleaning the bathroom may mean swabbing the toilet, polishing the mirror, and scrubbing the tub. To your spouse, it may mean flushing the toilet and straightening the towels.
- Lighten up. If you're overly proficient, why should your spouse struggle and stumble only to come up with second-rate results?
- Learn together. Community colleges have classes on organizing skills, clutter control, parenting, and the like. When we were expecting our first child, my husband and I took a parenting class together. The nurse-instructor showed us how, using lifelike dolls, to diaper, bathe, hold, and feed a newborn. Brilliant woman that she was, she enthusiastically encouraged and complimented the men who took it in like mother's milk. By the time she was finished with them, they could hardly wait to try their new skills on their own babies.
- If the results are shoddy, emphasize the economic advantages of doing the job properly: clothes last longer if they're washed right, flooring holds up better when it's maintained, there may be no need to pay an exterminator if the garbage is taken out every night. Money talks.

"Women, for hormonal reasons, can see individual dirt molecules, whereas men tend not to notice them until they join together into clumps large enough to support commercial agriculture."
—DAVE BARRY

SIGNING ON THE KIDS

Chores teach responsibility, self-discipline, time management, and a host of other values, believes family psychologist John Rosemond, lecturer and author of *To Spank or Not to Spank* and a series of other books on raising children.

"This isn't a matter of convenience or taking some burden off you," said Rosemond. "This is a matter of helping this child grow up to be a good citizen."

When children are allowed to take from the family more than they contribute, he maintains, they become parasitic, self-centered, and believe something can be had for nothing.

SEX AND HOUSEWORK

A Special Report *magazine poll of 555 married couples reveals the following:*

> • *Forty-two percent of the women said they'd prefer a clean house to an evening of lovemaking, 12 percent didn't know, while 64 percent of the men chose sex over the urge for order.*

> • *When asked if they'd rather marry a man who looks like Robert Redford but does no chores or marry a man who looks like Danny DeVito but does half the chores, 46 percent chose Redford and 43 percent chose DeVito.*

> • *Sixty-one percent said they found a man doing dishes more attractive than a man dancing nude, while 24 percent preferred dirty dancing to clean dishes.*

"There are three ways to get something done: do it yourself, employ someone, or forbid your children to do it."

—MONTA CRANE

"If you want a child to absorb your values," said Rosemond, "it's essential he or she contribute meaningfully to the family on a regular, daily basis."

It's best to start them young, but it's never too late to build a team mentality.

MOTIVATE

• Brainstorm. Hold monthly meetings at which family members make suggestions on the maintenance of the home.

•˙ Listen to all ideas. Because children aren't bound by habit, they can often come up with new solutions to old problems. "In the beginner's mind there are many possibilities," said a Japanese philosopher. "In the expert's there are few."

• Develop specialists. Teach one family member to be "the salad master," another "the omelet queen," another the "professional organizer."

• Feed the imagination. A "room captain" can "swab the decks," "run a tight ship," and keep the place "ship-

TEAM RULES

The McColl family relies on teamwork to keep their lives and their home in order. Emily and Duncan are full-time students at Princeton Theological Seminary and their four primary school–age children are involved in everything from playing a wide range of sports to studying Japanese.

"Everybody from the time they are four, has to get dressed and make his or her bed immediately after breakfast," said Emily. "Even when they were babies, they had to put their shoes in the closet. They'd often be in a heap, but at least they knew there was a home for everything."

Every night is pickup night, when all clutter is stashed in a big box before bedtime. "It doesn't matter if things are organized," said Emily. "The important thing is the floor is clear and we wake up to a tidy house."

Organization comes Saturday mornings when the entire family swarms through the house and puts everything in its place.

"The system works pretty well," said Emily. "The kids nag each other if someone leaves his socks or toys out. They're motivated because the sooner we're done, the sooner we can all go to the park."

To keep things running smoothly, the McColls post the following on the fridge:

THE HOUSEHOLD TEN COMMANDMENTS

1. *Respect other people—don't hurt them.*
2. *Respect others' things—don't break them.*
3. *Have your friends treat your house at least as well as they treat theirs.*
4. *Close all doors and cabinets (if it opens, it closes).*
5. *Leave shoes at the door.*
6. *Pick up after one activity before starting another.*
7. *Color only on paper.*
8. *Run and throw only outside.*
9. *Ask an adult permission to snack.*
10. *Sit to eat and drink and do it only at the table.*

shape." "Laundryman" can bust stains at a single stroke. "Highway patrol" can keep the floors debris- and dirt-free.

• Build pride. "Let's keep our home attractive, so our family and friends always feel good here."

• Blend the routine with the creative. Job instructions might read: "Please sweep the floor, wipe down the kitchen chairs, and pick a bouquet for the table." "Wash and vacuum the car and figure out how to make the interior smell better." "Clean out the fridge and see if you can create a meal out of what you find."

• Encourage imitation. Young children love to mimic their parents. Cut a mop and broom down to size, buy a stool for the sink, and encourage all attempts to clean.

• Offer rewards. The promise of an afternoon at the beach, park, or movies may motivate young procrastinators.

THE PLAN

• List chores. Some families use a job chart, others write household tasks on 3 × 5 cards and divide them among household members. When their children were young, John Rosemond and his wife, Willie, posted chores

---

JOB BENEFITS

According to a Harvard University study printed in Reader's Digest, *men who grew up doing regular chores around the house during the Great Depression were healthier, happier, and more successful in their adulthood jobs and families than those who didn't.*

The pattern ran true regardless of ethnic income, education, background, or family circumstances.

Researchers believe early successes at small chores inspired the men to tackle more and more challenging tasks, building their confidence and responsibility level till they were in a winning groove.

STARTING THEM EARLY

"You go into a nursery school and you'll see two- and three-year-olds pouring their own juice, making their own peanut butter sandwiches, and picking up their toys," said Dr. La Corte. "Yet we expect so little of them at home."

Nursery school director Carol Doughty agrees. "We teach the children to be self-sufficient here in the classroom, but as soon as Mom arrives, they become helpless again."

In order to ease them into chores early on, Doughty believes we ought to nurture children's love of playing house. Instead of plunking them down in front of the TV to get them out from under during meal preparation, we're better off teaching them how to break an egg, toast bread, stir a sauce, and other simple tasks. "Children love to cook," said Doughty. "That can be quality time for the two of you."

Preschoolers, she said, are also fascinated by anything to do with water: buckets, bubbles, sponges, and rubber gloves. She suggests providing a stool and letting them help wash dishes and wipe down counters in both the kitchen and bathroom. The results won't be spotless at first, but good habits will be established early on.

on a seven-day calendar on the fridge. "We found when chores were written, they became something that was not arguable, not optional. They were law. Family law."

• Train. Teaching takes time and patience, but the investment is rewarding for you and your child.

• Avoid gender jobs. "Women's work" went out with the corset. If Mom and Dad are democratic about job sharing, the kids won't get hung up on stereotyping. Girls can wax a car as well as boys can do the laundry.

• Define the time when a job is to be finished: before TV, phone calls, or lunch.

"A family is an organization. As such, everyone in the family should have the equivalent of a job description."
—JOHN ROSEMOND

THE PROCESS

• Use the answering machine to take messages during a cleaning session.

• Do it to music. Let them choose an upbeat tape or disc and boogie through the routine.

• Sell it as a workout. All that bending, stretching, and sweating is bound to tone the muscles and build strength.

• Break a big job into small segments. Cleaning out the garage may be overwhelming; tackling a corner of it is not.

• Don't redo a slipshod job. It sabotages your time and is hard on a child's self-esteem. Offer encouragement and show how to do the task, if necessary.

AVOIDING PROBLEMS

• Rotate jobs so no one gets stuck with the mundane and boring.

• Assign the responsibility. As soon as they get the hang of the job, give them the freedom of doing it their way.

• Get lost. Saturday mornings were squabble sessions at our house till I made myself scarce. I'd get up early, post a list, noting I looked forward to seeing the results at noon, and leave. It worked.

• Give fair warning. Flight attendant Lillian Palmer always calls her family from the airport when she comes in off a trip, saying she can hardly wait to see them and to relax in a clean, orderly home. "A little gift I've picked up along the way doesn't hurt either," said Palmer.

THE REALITY

• Don't expect miracles. Performance is more important than perfection.

• Keep things in perspective. The appearance of the home is probably more important to you than to anyone else in the household.

• Lower your standards. Better to have a comfortable home with a happy spouse and children than an immaculate showplace filled with neurotics. Lord knows, my family has helped lower mine.

ASSIGN AGE-APPROPRIATE TASKS

Start your kids early and have them work up to more challenging jobs as their confidence and ability develop.

"The more we capitalize on their own competence, the more competent they become, said John Rosemond. "It's in their own best interests."

A preschooler can:
- straighten a bed
- pick up and put away toys
- keep his or her room orderly
- feed the pets
- scrub vegetables
- separate dark laundry from light
- empty pockets
- match clean socks
- sweep a deck

An elementary-schooler can do all of the above as well as:
- set and clear a table (if the tableware is unbreakable)
- do the dishes
- unload the dishwasher
- dust furniture
- put away groceries
- prepare and pack his or her own school lunch
- empty wastebaskets
- take out the trash
- be in charge of recycling
- clean the bathroom sink and counter
- swab a toilet
- water a garden
- rake, jump in, and bag leaves
- shovel snow

A junior-high-schooler can do all of the above and:
- start dinner
- clean the refrigerator
- wash and vacuum floors
- polish furniture
- wash windows and polish mirrors
- clean a bathroom
- change a diaper
- change the sheets
- manually mow a lawn
- weed a garden
- wash a car

A high-schooler can do all of the above and:
- iron clothes
- cook dinner
- anything you can do, only not as well

Chapter 5

HIRING
A PRO

Once upon a time having household help was an indulgence reserved only for the rich, but today the professional house cleaner has become almost a necessity for those who have traded in their Pledge cans for paychecks.

Hairdresser Linda Frehe says she hired help when she first started working and moved in with a roommate.

"It cut down all the arguments about who does what when," she said. "The cleaner came in once a month, so it only cost us twenty dollars each. Whatever it costs, I'd rather work the extra hours than deal with the hassle."

Many, in fact, find paying someone else to scrub the toilets, tubs, and Tupperware is more than worth working a little overtime, or giving up a few meals out or weekends away.

The rewards are many:

- Home life is more harmonious since there's less nagging about chores and infractions.
- The whole place is clean at once.
- The job is better done.
- Hated tasks are a thing of the past.
- Weekends are free.
- There's more control over time.
- There's less wear and tear on the muscles.

"Housework is like cleaning fish. No matter how often you do it, it still stinks."

—THELMA HARPER IN "MAMA'S FAMILY"

- It raises standards, since everyone in the family knows how good their surroundings *can* look.

Having a pro may also promote better habits. The first time I hired someone, I ran through the house picking up and putting away out-of-place items so they wouldn't get lost and I wouldn't look like the slob that I am. By the time I finished, the house looked so good I would have canceled, had it not been for the layers of dust and the sticky floors. I use a pro only twice a month or less, but having one has gotten me into a fifteen-minute "scoop and stash" habit every morning.

INDEPENDENT VERSUS CLEANING SERVICE

An independent cleaner is almost always cheaper than a cleaning service, and you can train him or her your way, if that's important. Plus, an individual is often more flexible and willing to take on special jobs like ironing, laundry, starting dinner, and even baby-sitting.

A service provides the work you contract for, period. The rate is generally about 40 percent more than an independent's, but you can schedule work monthly, quarterly, or whenever you want it. The rates go up as the frequency goes down, however. A service will charge $70 for weekly cleaning, for instance, $85 every other week, $110 monthly, and $140 for an annual deep, heavy cleaning.

With a service, there's no lunch, transportation, training, firing, and can't-come-today annoyances. Also, a service generally provides all the equipment and is out of your house sooner, since there are often two or three to a team. Professional cleaner and *Speed Cleaning* author Jeff Campbell says his teams of three can clean a one-bedroom, one-bathroom house in about forty-seven minutes. The average independent needs at least four hours to do the same job.

The higher price a service charges may also be justified in the long run, since it generally takes care of insurance, taxes, and Social Security payments. A good agency will also provide only legally documented workers. So should you receive a political appointment, you don't have to worry about a "Nannygate" scandal.

"I think housework is the reason most women go to the office."
—HELOISE

It's crucial to check out an agency thoroughly, however, maintains Linda Radke, the former owner of a domestic employment agency and author of *Nannies, Maids & More* and *Cleaning Careers.*

"Just because you use an agency, it doesn't mean you're going to get the protection you're paying for," she said. "Ask questions. It's important to know you've got a good service agency behind you."

FINDING THE BEST

Whether you hire an independent or a service, the best way to find top help is to ask friends, colleagues, and neighbors whose standards are equal to or better than yours for their recommendations.

Even if a service does come highly recommended, look for one that's been established for at least two years. Cleaning businesses have a higher than average failure rate, and you don't want to be left in the lurch the day you host the party of the year or put your house on the market.

Monique Milliman, owner and operator of The Dirt Busters, a California house-cleaning service, says to look for the following when checking out a company:

- An in-home estimate. "A phone estimate is useless unless they can guarantee the price," said Milliman.
- A detailed list of what's included in the cleaning.
- That equipment and supplies are provided.
- That all help are on the payroll. If they're not, they may not be insured or bonded and could be illegal aliens.
- Teams of two or more. "Teams are more efficient and thorough," explained Milliman. "You've got more than one set of eyes to catch things."

• That there's a working supervisor, someone who is actually in charge.

THE AD

If you don't know anyone who employs a house cleaner and you don't want to pay the price of a service, posting an ad on the community bulletin board and/or running one in the local paper is an alternative.

You'll need to include the following:

• Job description
• Location
• Days and hours
• Wages
• Whether or not smoking is acceptable

Make it brief, explicit, and to-the-point. Example:

Housecleaner. 8 hours weekly. Day & hours flexible. Must have own car, local references. Nonsmoking. Springfield. $50. 555-2113.

Tip: Don't hire someone to work on Mondays. There are too many legal holidays to deal with.

INTERVIEWING THE INDEPENDENT

Ask about their work experience, why they left their last job, if that's the case, and look for ability, maturity, and enthusiasm. If their references check out, offer a few trial sessions before you commit.

TRAINING THE INDEPENDENT

It's always a good idea to write out the job description, prepare a room-by-room list of items and surfaces to be

cleaned, and to actually walk through the whole place noting any fragile items and vulnerable surfaces. If they're
inexperienced, it might be necessary to work alongside
them the first time or two.

    Once they get the hang of it, assign the responsibility.
It's hard for cleaners to take pride in their work when the
boss is looking over their shoulders telling them how to
arrange the books or fluff the pillows. My cleaning
woman, Juana, always neatly folds the blankets I like artfully tossed over the arms of the sofa and chairs. She also
lines up the kitchen chairs on the diagonal, while I like
them square. She does such a splendid job cleaning, I let
her play house while she's at it. It's no big deal to change
things after she's out the door.

    If the work is good, say so. If it isn't, point out the
problem, make suggestions, and show how, if necessary.
Be positive and expect the best and you'll likely get it.

*"Just give me the
luxuries of life; I can
live without the
necessities."*

—OSCAR WILDE

HOLDING ON TO GOOD HELP

Some people hang on to their help for decades, while others go through them like rolls of paper towels. It helps to
pay a little more than the going rate to keep good help. And
treating your help with respect and dignity promotes loy-
alty and a willingness to go the extra mile.

    The following are gestures independent cleaners say
they'd most like from their employers:

- The offer of a cup of tea or coffee on arrival
- Asking for lunch preferences and providing them
- Keeping equipment in good repair in an accessible
  spot
- Asking if there's a preference for a specific mop,
  cleaner, and the like
- Replenishing supplies when needed
- Restricting the movement of pets and people during
  cleaning hours

- Picking up loose items so there's more time spent cleaning and less shuffling the watchamacallits
- Appreciation for specific jobs well done
- Providing appropriate bonuses and raises
- Presenting a small gift at the holidays

Kindness and thoughtfulness foster a sense of belonging with help, maintains Linda Radke. "They feel they're not just cleaning your house, they feel needed and appreciated," she said. "Everybody needs that."

THE SEMIPRO

If a professional doesn't fit the budget, consider hiring a high school or college student either to help with the overall cleaning or to take on specific jobs like scrubbing floors or washing windows. Since they're mostly young and inexperienced, it's a good idea to assign them relatively brainless jobs where the damage factor is low. Polishing the silver and cleaning out the dog run, for instance, are safe; ironing the silk and washing the Baccarat are not.

Another possibility is to pay the sitter extra to do chores after the kids are in bed. A few bites out of the weekly workload can make a world of difference.

TIME AND CONVENIENCE SERVICES

There's a lot more to running a house than cleaning it. There's food to be bought, dogs to be groomed, paperwork to be filed, and all the dumb but demanding details that rob us of time for the things we really want to do. And it's not getting any easier timewise. Harris polls show our working hours have increased by 20 percent in the last eighteen years while our leisure time has dropped by 32 percent. There's just too much to do and too little time to do it in.

"The time crunch is grabbing everyone by the jugular," said Joyce Poe, owner of Services Poe-Pourri, one of the many personal service companies popping up around the country.

These convenience peddlers are made up of professional shoppers, organizers, and errand runners who will do everything from ferrying puppy poop to the vet to making you look like Martha Stewart at your next party.

They're set up to help you out for either a one-shot event or on a regular basis. Some are listed in the Yellow Pages under "Personal Services," while others can only be found word-of-mouth.

As with all help, request references and check them out. Also ask for a brochure and see how long it takes to arrive. If they aren't organized enough to get their own materials in the mail, it's doubtful they're going to get your life into shape.

Most claim to "do everything," but like the rest of us, each has his or her strengths and weaknesses. Some are accomplished cooks and can whip up intimate dinners or cater big events. Others shine in office skills and checkbook balancing but have the taste of Peg Bundy when it comes to shopping.

Think about jobs you hate to do, as well as chores that infringe on family and career. Then look for someone whose skills and background are up to the challenge.

As for price, ask for an estimate of the jobs you have in mind, and check to see if gasoline mileage is included in the price. And negotiate. The rates quoted aren't carved in stone, as the head of one service confided.

Also consider:
- Dry cleaners and laundries that fetch and deliver
- Restaurants, delis, and markets that deliver
- Banks that pay your bills
- Gardeners or a teenager who will weed and haul
- Pool cleaners
- Specialty cleaners like window washers, furniture and carpet shampooers, and floor polishers

SHALLOW POCKETS

Some people get around the cost problem by bartering their talents with others. I know of a writer who writes the brochures and magazine ads for a commercial janitorial service in exchange for weekly house cleaning. I've heard of others trading their culinary skills with a friend who would rather clean than cook.

It's common practice in some neighborhoods to provide room and board in the guest house or an empty bedroom in exchange for one day of cleaning. It leaves the boarder free the rest of the week to pursue other jobs.

The point is you don't have to be wealthy to avoid the crud detail. Often all it takes is a little resourcefulness and ingenuity.

Part II

CLEARING
CLEANING
HURDLES

Chapter 6

GUESTAPHOBIA

Like migrating geese, guests start flying in when the weather warms, often settling in near a body of water, though they're known to adapt to most locations.

It's illegal to shoot them and impolite to shoo them away, so we have to know how to handle them without ruffling their feathers or working off our own.

"Tact is the art of making your guests feel at home when that's where you wish they really were."

—George Bergman

PRACTICING SELECTIVE HOSPITALITY

• Think twice before casually tossing off invitations. After sharing dinner, a bottle of wine, and a "Come and see us sometime" with a couple of American backpackers in Spain, Connie and Sam Ellis found one of them on their doorstep a few months later. He turned out to be the guest from hell, and by the end of the summer he practically had to be evicted from their house.

• Be assertive. Judith Martin, better known as "Miss Manners," believes in what she calls "preventative hospitality," maintaining anyone we know well enough to bed down we should also know well enough to ask, "How long will you stay?" And if the timing is not convenient, to say, "That's not a good time for us." "It's better to bar the door to unwanted guests than to back them out through it," she writes in her *Miss Manners' Guide to Excruciatingly Correct Behavior.*

"You are leaving Sunday, aren't you?"
—WHAT TO EMBROIDER ON A GUEST ROOM PILLOW

• Know your limit. That might be one night in your situation, two weeks in someone else's. Just keep in mind that short visits make long friendships.

INTEGRATING THEM INTO THE HOUSEHOLD

• Get them involved. Most people are grateful when they're made to feel useful. When you hear "Can I help?" instead of the usual "No, that's OK," be ready with "Sure, you can play with the baby," "Set the table," or "Toss the salad." They'll feel part of the family, and you'll feel less put out.

• Show them how. Private tutor Julia Sweeney practices her "Queen for a Day" approach when she has guests. She coddles them the first day, settling them in and making company meals. After dinner she gives an in-depth tour, introducing them to the coffeemaker, fridge, washer, and dryer, telling them "*Mi* appliances *es su* appliances." She's found her guests not only appreciate being self-sufficient but sometimes reciprocate by tossing the family laundry in the washer with their own load and cooking breakfast for everyone.

SLEEPING ARRANGEMENTS

Back in the Dark Ages, sleeping arrangements were simple, since everyone just bedded down with the dogs in front of the fire. Today, unfortunately, we're expected to provide more in the way of comfort.

• If there's a guest room, make it as self-sufficient as possible, with reading material, good light, extra blankets, and a comfortable chair, so it's an escape valve for everyone.

• If drawer space is already cramped, provide a folding luggage rack.

• Keep extra hangers in the closet so there's no scrounging around for them at the last minute. Buy them in a special color so they get put back where they belong.

CHOOSING THE PERFECT SOFA BED

• *Before you shop at the local couch-a-rama, measure the space in which the sofa is to fit. Sleep sofas come with mattresses from twin to king size. They take about three feet of depth closed and up to a little over seven feet when opened.*

• *Consider a couple of chair-sized twin sleepers over one sofa-sized unit for versatility. Not all couples want to sleep in the same bed.*

• *Bring surrounding paint chip samples and fabric swatches to the store to make sure the upholstery color will work well with your decor.*

• *Choose tightly woven fabric in color and print that camouflages soil.*

• *Avoid a striped fabric on a special-order piece. The stripes on the cushions may line up with the body of the sofa on the showroom model, but they often come in unmatched from the factory.*

• *Make sure sofa cushions are reversible for longer wear.*

• *Sit on the cushions. They should be deep enough to accommodate your thigh to where the knee bends, and dense enough to provide comfortable back and buttock support.*

• *Ask the seller about the frame. Kiln-dried hardwood is best, since it won't warp. Softwood, particle board, and plastic probably will.*

• *Pull out the mattress to see if the metal mechanism slides easily. Even if the showroom floor is cramped, don't take the seller's word for ease of operation. All mechanisms are not created equal.*

• *Lie and roll around on the mattress, preferably with a partner. Is it comfortable? Does it dip in the middle? Does the frame squeak and wobble?*

• *Sit on the foot of the bed to see if the center support legs leave the floor. They shouldn't.*

• *Look on a sofa bed as a compromise. Since it's a hybrid, it won't be quite as comfortable as a conventional sofa or a bed. But it will fill the bill if space is tight.*

• If Auntie Ruth or Grandma is to share space with one of the children, give the child some control over the situation by letting her decide which drawers should be used, which sheets would be the "coolest," and maybe which stuffed animal would look best on the guest's bed.

• Provide synthetic and cotton bedding instead of wool, feathers, and down. Cotton and synthetic blankets and pillows won't provoke allergies and are easier to keep clean.

• Provide guests with a simple-to-use alarm clock so you won't have to worry about their early appointments.

• If there's no guest room, a Hide-A-Bed, daybed, or wall bed can come to the rescue. The wall bed, an updated version of the original Murphy bed, folds up in its own cabinet, so it takes up minimal floor space.

• If the budget is tight, a futon or an air mattress can do the job without making guests so comfortable they'll want to settle in long-term.

• Don't worry about bedding down children. Snuggling into sleeping bags almost anywhere is an adventure for most, especially if they can do it under the stars or on the floor in front of an entertaining video.

• Buy or borrow a small inflatable wading pool for a baby's bed and bathtub.

• Use a folding screen when guests bed down in the living room, to ensure privacy and to set a boundary for spreading belongings.

• Provide a flashlight, so maneuvering from bed to bath is safe in the dead of night. You don't want a convalescent on your hands for another week.

THE BATHROOM

• Issue guests a set of towels in a different color from the family's to prevent mix-ups.

• Keep in reserve a few towels and a fresh bar of soap in a basket or caddy to keep for future guests. Leave space for their own paraphernalia so they can tote it in and out of the bathroom.

FEEDING

• Keep it simple, but give it flair. An easy dish like broiled fish can be dressed up with a garnish of crushed macadamia nuts and served on a bed of greens. Spoon a dollop of sour cream and caviar on a baked potato. A plain green salad can look like a Martha Stewart special with a sprinkling of edible flowers.

"Staying with people consists of your not having your way and their not having theirs."
—MAARTEN MAARTENS

- Stock up on make-ahead dishes: pasta salads, casseroles, roasted chicken or turkey breast, lasagna, chili, soups, and stews.
- Throw some meat and veggies in the slow cooker. They'll be dinner by the time you get home from work or a day of touring.
- Post a list on the fridge as to what meal and snack items are inside.
- Leave around a few idiotproof recipes and hope your guests make dinner for you.
- Keep a bowl of fresh fruit on the table for snacking.
- Stop off at the local deli, Asian, or fast-food restaurant. Takeout has saved the sanity of many a host.
- Make the farmer's market and gourmet grocer part of the local tour to save a marketing trip.
- Cut down on dishwashing with disposable plates, cups, and glasses.
- Eat out. With any luck, guests will share or pick up the tab.

MAKING CLEANUP EASIER

- Make it easy for guests to clean up after themselves by keeping cleaning supplies in the bathroom and a squeegee in the shower.

HOW ABOUT A LITTLE COLD SHOULDER?

According to Charles Panati, author of Extraordinary Origins of Everyday Things, *"giving someone the cold shoulder" or snub comes from the medieval custom of serving a guest who had overstayed his or her welcome nothing but roasted cold shoulder of beef. Supposedly after a steady diet of cold shoulder, the guest would take the hint and depart.*

• Post house rules concerning smoking, where to hang wet swimsuits, and such. Go for the humorous approach, and place the list somewhere unobtrusive but hard to miss, like behind the bathroom door.

• Laminate and hang clear, detailed instructions on how to operate the washing machine.

• Leave a clean set of sheets out the night before departure and hope guests take the hint and make the bed in the morning.

CHILDPROOFING

• If there are small children in the entourage, protect the upholstery with washable throws and the mattresses with vinyl liners. Also stash fragile items and keep medicines, cleaning equipment, and other chemicals out of reach.

• Place plenty of premoistened pop-up towels around the house.

• Keep small hands out of big trouble by laying in a supply of age-appropriate games, coloring books, crayons, puzzles, and videos. Bring out only one or two items at a time. Children become distracted and bored with too many choices.

• Serve nonstaining drinks, like ice water, lemonade, and clear soda.

ENTERTAINING

• Realize you don't need to take on the role of social director. I used to plan a full schedule for my mother when she visited, only to find she was exhausted by the time she left. It took me a while to figure she came to see me more than the sights and was happier playing with the grandchildren than she was playing the tourist.

• Provide a supply of local guidebooks, maps, train

and bus schedules, local tour information, etc., so guests can take the initiative if they want to.

• Let guests know that dishwashing is an accepted form of entertainment.

• Stock up on some good mysteries, juicy novels, or whatever you think your guests like to read to keep them occupied.

• Order an extra newspaper for the duration. You'll have yours, they'll have theirs, and you won't have to make polite conversation for at least an hour.

"The most charming visitor may linger one day too long. The best time to go is when everyone's asking you to stay."
—ELIZA C. HALL

DARK SECRETS

Overnight and long-term guests are bound to discover that the medicine cabinet hasn't been cleared since the Carter administration, that the oven hasn't been scrubbed since last Thanksgiving, and that every drawer in the house is a junk drawer. Rather than fret over it, realize:

MEETING ON NEUTRAL GROUND

Lauren and Rosie are sisters, both in their seventies, who are close but haven't visited each other's homes in over twenty years.

"Our husbands are not overly fond of each other," says Rosie, who lives in Vancouver; her sister, Lauren, lives in northern California.

"We don't appreciate each other's lifestyle either," says Lauren. "She's in bed every night after dinner, while I like to party. The last time I visited Rosie, she practically starved me, served me cheap Scotch, and not much of it, and left me to my own devices every evening. It was awful."

But the sisters have found a way to visit without the grief. They meet for an annual week together at Rancho La Puerta, a luxurious health spa in Tecate, Mexico.

"It's neutral territory," says Lauren. "We work out, relax, and eat together, and do our own thing when we want, without putting each other out."

- It's a rare individual who doesn't have some real or imagined housekeeping skeleton in his or her closet.
- Your housekeeping deficits make you more endearing and down-to-earth and less intimidating.
- Since you are making your guests feel superior about their own cleaning and organizing skills, they'll be more apt to invite you as a guest into their own homes.

Chapter 7

FIFTY WAYS (MORE OR LESS) TO LOSE YOUR CLUTTER

They say you can't take it with you when you go to heaven, but rumor is if you go to hell, you not only take it with you but spend eternity sorting, scrubbing, and polishing it.

"Life is 5 percent joy, 5 percent grief, and 90 percent maintenance."
—HARRIET SCHECHTER, PROFESSIONAL ORGANIZER

To avoid hell on earth, we need to take a long, hard look at the stuff Clutter King Don Aslett says we spend half our time accumulating and the other half maintaining; the stuff that makes a clean home look messy and a dirty home a disaster.

PUBLIC ENEMY NUMBER 1: PAPER

When professional organizer Harriet Schechter polls her "Letting Go of Clutter" workshop students on their biggest clutter problem, 95 percent say it's paper. "We're inundated with it today," says Schechter, co-author of *More Time for Sex: The Organizing Guide for Busy Couples.* "We've become information junkies, but we can't begin to read everything that comes across our desks or through the mail."

Schechter suggests keeping paper under control by remembering the 3-Ds: do it, delegate it, or dump it.

• Think of the wastebasket as an ally in the war against paper. "Treat them like babies," advises Schechter. "Keep them within easy reach, feed them regularly, and change them often."

• Consolidate bills by using one major credit card. By retiring department and specialty-store cards, we also remove our names from mailbox-clogging ads.

• Find a bank that will pay regular bills like mortgage, utility, insurance, and car payments automatically. You'll not only cut down on mail, you'll cut down on check writing, envelope addressing, and stamps.

• Have the bank pay sometime bills as well. You just phone in and enter your access number and secret code. Your bank statement will provide the legal record of all payments.

• See if your bank offers check imaging. Instead of a bundle of canceled checks to wade through and store, you get miniaturized pictures of each check printed right on your statement.

• Take a bite out of junk mail by removing your name from direct-marketing lists that include mail-order companies, financial services, subscription offers, sweepstakes, and other national mailings. Write to:

> Mail Preference Service
> Direct Marketing Association
> P.O. Box 9008
> Farmingdale, NY 11735-9008

The Mail Preference Service's "delete file" is made available quarterly to business subscribers who want to get the most bang for the buck. Names of uninterested consumers are maintained for five years, after which you'll need to reregister. Business-to-business letters, charitable requests, and "resident" or "occupant" addressed mailings aren't affected, but MPS says you'll notice a considerable drop in nationally generated third-class mail in about three months.

• Request favorite catalog companies not to sell your name to other mailers.

• Be discriminating about entering sweepstakes and contests, ordering merchandise, and filling out "reader request" questionnaires.

KILLER CLUTTER

Clutter can be hazardous to your mental and physical health. It has caused fights, divorce, anxiety, alienation, injury, and even death.

Take the case of the San Bernardino, California, man who makes the rounds of garage sales, flea markets, and dumps every weekend, foraging treasure. Now that his house, garage, and yard are full, he's draining the swimming pool to contain yet more goods. His wife is threatening divorce.

Then there's Anthony Cima, an 87-year-old San Diego man critically injured when his book collection buried him during a 1986 earthquake. Cima was pinned to his cot for eleven hours in his tiny rented room when his towering stacks of 10,000 books toppled on him.

Perhaps the most notorious clutter-gone-berserk case was that of the Collyer brothers in 1947. Each room in their three-story New York brownstone was stacked floor-to-ceiling with a forty-year collection of newspapers, magazines, mail, and everything else that came through the door. Only narrow paths snaked through the debris from one room to the next.

They found the body of 65-year-old heart-attack victim Homer first. But it took authorities weeks to find 61-year-old Langley, who had been crushed by a tumbling pile of junk.

- Open bills immediately, and toss out the outside envelopes and accompanying propaganda.
- Bag it. When a desk or table overflows with mail, sort the mail, then stuff it in a good-looking gift or shopping bag and deal with it in regular sessions of fifteen to twenty minutes.
- Patronize the library. Most carry a good selection of local and national newspapers, magazines, and journals. You can read the noncirculating material in relative peace and quiet and check out just what you have time to read when you have time to read it.
- For the periodicals you do buy, rip out the articles of interest and can the rest. I tear and staple compact *Reader's Digest* stories, stuff them in a self-sealing plastic sandwich bag, and keep them in the door-well of my car to read when I'm delayed somewhere.

"He who knows he has enough is rich."

—Lao-tzu

• Share books. Many of us believe we can never have too many, but when shelves sag and stalagmites of volumes rise from the floor, either peddle them to a secondhand-book store, donate them to a library book sale, or give them away to friends.

• Chuck catalogs immediately if nothing catches your cyc on the first browse through. Hold on to them if there are potential possibilities, but only for a short time. Mail-order merchandise is phased out at least seasonally, so if you wait longer than a few months, chances are the item won't be available.

GADGETS, GIZMOS, AND WATCHAMACALLITS

• Before cluttering up a counter, desk, or worktable with yet another "timesaving convenience" ask yourself if the item is worth the space, cleaning, and maintenance. Is a toaster oven necessary when the big oven can do the job *and* hide the crud? Is an automatic pencil sharpener crucial when you mainly write with pens? Will an electric nail buffer add to the quality of life?

• Chuck stuff beyond repair: the rusty can opener, the cracked tape recorder, the unreliable alarm clock. They may have cost good money, but they're now junking up good space.

• Rent—don't own. There comes a time when we may need a sequined ball gown, a fifty-cup coffeemaker, or a tree pruner with a cat-rescue noose. Renting occasional-use items is not only cheaper than buying, there's no worry about dust, rust, and obsolescence.

• Borrow. There are some tightly knit neighborhoods that share everything from paint sprayers to floor polishers. Organize your own block or building of willing sharers, so no one storage space is ever too cluttered with gizmos.

CLOTHES

When our size 8s no longer fit our size-12 bodies, our disco duds no longer suit our buttoned-down image, and our closets suffer from clothestrophobia, maybe it's time to move 'em on out.

"Never love anything that can't love you back."
—DON ASLETT

- Consider selling good but outgrown clothes at a consignment shop.
- Set up a swap box. Registered nurse Sylvia Taddish established a swap closet in the common room of her Wheeling, Illinois, apartment complex, where residents anonymously trade their castoffs for others. Sylvia gives but seldom receives. "It feels so good to clean out a space that I don't want to add any more," she says. "It's like losing weight. Going back to the junk only starts the whole cycle again."
- Donate items to charity. Churches, shelters, as well as Goodwill Industries, the St. Vincent de Paul Society, and the Salvation Army are glad to get clean, wearable items for the needy. Keeping someone less fortunate warm while simplifying our own lives is a winning combination.

TOYS

We may think we're buying ourselves time with another toy to entertain Junior, but we usually end up picking up and tripping up over a carpet bristling with plastic.

- Hide and rotate toys a few at a time. Interest cools with too many, and pickup is time-consuming.
- Avoid buying toys with hundreds of tiny pieces that are easily lost in the carpet and painfully found in the feet.
- Instead of buying more toys, videos, and computer games, encourage children to nurture friendships, join Scouts, take up a sport, and use their imaginations.
- For birthdays and holidays, give the gift of yourself to a child: a weekend camping, a day fishing, an after-

noon flying a kite in the park will be more cherished in the long run than another trinket or toy.

GIFTS

• Give adults experiences, not things: a gift certificate for a massage, a day at a spa, a weekend at a B&B are often more appreciated than more stuff to store and maintain.

• Ask for the above when you're the recipient.

• Bring home edible travel souvenirs to your kids, friends, and the neighbor who fed your cat. Regional specialties like macadamia nuts from Hawaii, dark chocolate from Belgium, coffee beans from Costa Rica provide a sensory link to a place and don't take up space or need to be dusted.

FURNISHINGS

• Adopt the "Bare Is Beautiful" look. Surfaces clear of mail, magazines, and knickknacks are easier to maintain and make a room seem more serene.

• Don't confuse *House Beautiful* with *House Clutterful*. Those country cottages chock-full of collections may look cozy, but they demand constant care.

• Choose size over quantity. One good-sized table backing a sofa is more effective than a scattering of tiny tables around the room.

• Capitalize on storage capabilities. A chest at the foot of the bed is more serviceable than a bench, a vanity sink is more practical than a pedestal model, a desk with built-in file drawers is better than a slim-legged one with a few shallow drawers.

• Realize you need to allocate space and maintenance time to anything brought into the home, whether it's a new sofa or an old sideboard.

• Remove temptation. If a piece is a catchall for junk, move it elsewhere or get rid of it altogether. When my daughter Lisa got in the habit of dumping her books, papers, and other debris on a tea cart in the kitchen, I relegated the piece to the living room as a lamp table. She had to unload in her room instead, where the rest of us didn't have to deal with it.

• Get rid of area rugs that serve no real purpose. Bare floors are easier to care for.

• Focus on what counts: comfortable seating, good lighting, and plenty of work and play space. The rest is icing on the cake, and too much of it can make us sick.

FLOTSAM AND JETSAM

• Anchor items that frequently disappear. Provide a hook by the door for car keys, a standing eyeglass case on the desk, a pen tied to the phone cord.

• Set aside five to ten minutes at the end of every day to file and straighten out a desk, so there's no morning mess to face.

JUST DO IT

Perhaps the biggest challenge to conquering clutter is finding the time and the energy to deal with it.

• *Don't wait for the perfect moment or a big block of time. It may never come. Clutter needs to be dealt with daily, a little at a time.*

• *Set up for a dreaded job ahead of time, bringing in a trash can, sacks, and cardboard boxes. A job started is a job halfway done.*

• *Start with an area that bugs you the most—a littered garage, for instance. For instant gratification, begin with an easily organized corner.*

• *Set the kitchen timer so you don't get burned out on a clutter-cleaning frenzy.*

• *Make it pleasant. Slip a tape into your radio or Walkman and toss to Mozart or Michener.*

• *Do it regularly, and think of clutter control as a work in progress, not something that gets done once and stays neat forever.*

How Cluttered Are You?

Questions:
1. *Do you see clutter as a permanent part of the decor?*
2. *Do you prefer the country look because of its emphasis on clutter?*
3. *Have you ever found it easier to go out and buy a new something or other because it was too much trouble to look through the rubble for the old one?*
4. *Do you periodically move things from room to room 'cause you can't figure out what to do with them?*
5. *Do you hang on to bad books, boring videos, outgrown toys, and out-of-style clothes?*
6. *Are you too ashamed to have visitors or even repairmen in because of your accumulation of stuff?*
7. *Have you ever missed an appointment because you couldn't find your calendar?*
8. *Do you hold on to something you don't use because you or somebody might need it "someday"?*
9. *Do you rent storage space for items you know you'll never use?*
10. *Do you own appliances, power tools, and cars that don't work anymore?*
11. *Do you start new projects before you finish old ones?*
12. *Do you avoid tackling a messy garage, room, cabinet, or drawer because there's never enough time?*
13. *Does your desk sport the layered look, with bills on the bottom, memos in the middle, and unopened mail on top?*
14. *Do you spend your free time frequenting garage sales, flea markets, and swap meets?*
15. *Is shopping a passion?*
16. *Do you view the dump as a vast field of dreams?*
17. *Has the junk in your junk drawer multiplied and grown like mold into surrounding areas?*
18. *If you had the opportunity to move to the home of your dreams, a home with a fabulous view, a convenient location, and an award-winning design, would you turn down the chance if it lacked existing and potential storage space for all your stuff?*
19. *If you had to move, would it take you more than a month to pack your possessions?*

20. *Do you squirrel away motley possessions in hopes that they might be valuable one day?*
21. *Is it difficult to close the door to your closet because it's bulging with belongings?*
22. *Would you be embarrassed to have people paw through your things if you were incapacitated for a time?*
23. *Do you buy things you don't really want to impress people you don't really like?*
24. *Do you buy stuff on sale only because it's a bargain?*
25. *Do you feel your stuff controls you rather than the other way around?*

How to Score:
- *Count all your "Yeses."*
- *One to five: You're practically perfect. Consider a career shaping up others less organized.*
- *Six to ten: You're organizationally challenged, but with effort, time, and tossing, there's hope.*
- *Eleven to seventeen: You're debris-dysfunctional. Call in a professional organizer to help clear and organize spaces, provide ideas, recommend organizing equipment, and set up filing systems. Check the Yellow Pages under "Organizing Services" or "Personal Services."*
- *Eighteen to twenty-five: You suffer from possession obsession. Consider Messies Anonymous, a support group for packrats, or Clutterers Anonymous, a self-help group based on a 12-step program. For a group near you, or information about organizing your own group, write:*

Messies Anonymous
Dept. B
5025 SW 114th Avenue
Miami, FL 33165
(Founder Sandra Felton is also organizing support groups for families of messies.)

Clutterers Anonymous
World Service Organization
P.O. Box 25884
Santa Ana, CA 92799-5884
(Send $1 and a self-addressed, stamped envelope.)

• Hide it. Toss housemates' out-of-place belongings in a big box somewhere a bit inconvenient to retrieve.

• Take a picture. Those baby clothes, dried corsages, and travel souvenirs may be hard to part with, but if you photograph them before you pack them off, their sentimental value is always with you.

• Give it back. When the kids grow up, move out, and leave their things behind, humorist Andy Rooney suggests sneaking their stuff into their car trunks and under their seats while they're inside visiting. "Eventually," explained Rooney on a *60 Minutes* commentary, "you'll have enough room inside to store more of your own stuff."

• Sell it. A garage sale is a dandy way of shedding stuff and getting paid for it. Make it a neighborhood affair to enlist help and attract a bigger crowd.

• Bestow it. When collections run amok, see if a museum or a library is interested. When my husband's passion for old cars got out of hand, he (or maybe it was I) was delighted to find the local auto museum not only gave him a nice tax deduction but displayed his babies and gave him full visitation rights. You can also loan an item or a collection if you're not quite ready to say good-bye.

• Give it away. Prevent a hauling hernia by putting a large item on the lawn with a big "free" sign. There are enough human pack rats out there who can't resist another thingamajig. Their gain is your freedom.

Chapter 8

ESCAPING THE LAUNDRY

In days of old, wash day was all day, and caustic soaps, boiling, and wringing by hand took their toll on the laundry and laundress alike. On top of that, heavy irons were heated in the fire or on the stove, and clothes and hands were frequently scorched.

"Time given to thought is the greatest time saver of all."
—NORMAN COUSINS

Today, clothes care is a relative walk in the park, aided by the washer, dryer, and steam iron. But if you've ever faced mountains of wash and baskets of wrinkled garments on the morning when everyone has run out of underwear and clean shirts, you know there's still plenty of room for improvement.

The trick is to get the household involved in the process. Family members are less apt to toss hardly worn and used items in the bin if they know they have to wash, dry, and unwrinkle them themselves.

In my case, I got the family involved through my own incompetence. When they complained of missing socks and mixed wardrobes, I made them see there would be fewer problems if they cared for their own clothes. My husband was a hard sell, but I convinced him that anyone who could come off an Air Force mission, jump in the shower, flight suit and all, dry out, and fly was resourceful enough to use a washer and dryer.

SETTING UP SHOP

To ease everyone into the act, the laundry area should be convenient and user-friendly:

- If instructions aren't printed on the washer lid, type, laminate, and hang them over the machine.
- Install a shelf over the washer and dryer, so detergent, bleach, and other necessities are within easy reach.
- Make sure all surfaces are waterproof and easy to maintain: plastic laminate counters, gloss or semi-gloss latex walls, and no-wax vinyl floors.
- Paint walls white. Colored walls can reflect strange tones on laundry.
- Hang a drip-dry rod over the sink, slip a clothes caddy over the door, and nail an expanding wooden peg rack on the wall.
- Provide a large enough counter or table for sorting, stain-treating, and folding. If space is tight, a drop-down, wall-hinged table will do the trick.
- Use a white bin for whites, a bright bin for colors, and a small bin for delicates.
- Label or color-code bedroom baskets to prevent laundry-room mix-ups.
- Combine strong overhead with wall or undershelf lights for stain-busting, mending, and separating black from navy socks. Regular incandescent light-bulbs are best, since fluorescent bulbs tend to gray whites.

SPOT AND STAIN PREVENTION

- Wear a T-shirt, a cotton camisole, or dress shields under good clothes to absorb perspiration.
- Change from good clothes into comfortable knock-abouts as soon as you get home.
- Get into the habit of wearing an apron or work shirt while cooking and doing messy projects.

- Wear a bib or a big bandanna when eating sloppy foods like boiled lobster, fried chicken, and spaghetti.
- Let deodorant and fragrance dry thoroughly before dressing.
- Make use of the sun. Turn slightly sweaty but not yet dirty clothes inside out and deodorize them in strong sunlight.
- Use the model's trick of covering a made-up face with an old scarf before slipping a garment over the head. Or dress first and protect clothes from renegade makeup by tying the scarf around your neck.
- Keep purses and briefcases off the floor, since they can soil clothes as they brush against them.
- Buy silk shirts on the large side to avoid tight-armhole sweat stains.
- Spray fabric protector on raincoats, canvas shoes, cotton neckties, and scarfs. Test first on an inconspicuous spot.

> *"I love doing laundry. I even make it up; I mean, I throw things on the floor to make laundry. That's how much I love it."*
> —WHOOPI GOLDBERG

DAMAGE CONTROL

- Dissolve detergent, bleach, and water softener in the wash water before loading clothes.
- Wash and dry clothes inside out to prevent fading.
- Tie or pin socks together for easier sorting.
- Clean washer hoses of hardened soap scum by running an empty load with hot water and a cup or so of distilled vinegar.
- Prevent tangling by closing zippers, buttoning but-

EQUAL OPPORTUNITY

When British prime minister Margaret Thatcher and her husband, Denis, moved into the official residence at 10 Downing Street, a reporter asked Denis Thatcher, "Who wears the pants in this house?" He answered, "I do. And I also wash and iron them."

tons, and tying strings before they go into the washer and dryer.

- Avoid the contortions of folding clean sheets by putting them right back on the bed.
- If there's no in-house water softener and the water is full of laundry-graying minerals, use a powdered softener like Calgon or White King.
- Pilling is caused by items' rubbing against each other in the washer and dryer. Prevent it by turning susceptible clothes inside out and washing them in a mesh bag or a drawstring pillowcase.
- If you're the chief washer, buy one distinctive style, pattern, or color of socks and underwear for each member of the household to prevent mixing and ease matching.
- Buy enough of the above to get everyone through at least a week.
- Mark labels with different-colored laundry pens to keep everyone's clothes separate.

AN EASIER APPROACH TO COMING CLEAN

- Wash pantyhose with shampoo as you wash your hair in the shower and you'll always have a clean pair. Bras and silk panties can join you too.
- Hang a mesh laundry bag inside a closet door for hand washables. Toss the bag in the washer set on the

---

IT'S TIME TO JOB-SHARE WHEN

- *The kids change outfits four times a day.*
- *Dirty socks are left on the floor for you to pick up.*
- *Towels end up in the basket after only one shower.*
- *Bedroom baskets are filled with both clean and dirty clothes because their wearers were too lazy to put them away last week.*
- *You change the sheets of anyone over age five but your own.*

FIVE WAYS TO FOIL LINT

1. Separate "lint donors" like towels and flannels from "lint recipients" like washable velvet, corduroy, knits, and some synthetics.
2. Wash and dry dark items separately from light ones.
3. Toss a yard of nylon netting in the dryer.
4. Clean the lint filter before or after every load.
5. Use a lint brush instead of tape; tape leaves a sticky residue that attracts more lint.

---

delicate, cold-water cycle. Machine washing beats manual dunking, swishing, and squeezing.

- Instead of washing, have the dryer dust throw pillows, curtains, and slipcovers. Set it on cool, toss in a big towel as a buffer and a fabric softener sheet as a sweetener.
- Make doing the wash less of a big deal. Toss in a load while cooking supper, paying bills, or reading the paper, so it won't mount up and become a weekend chore.

FREEDOM FROM THE PRESS

Ironing is not only a time waster, it is almost as hard on clothes as dry cleaning, since it weakens and dries out fibers.

- Shop for knits, heavily textured sweaters, lined wool, corduroy, crushed velvet, seersucker, piqué, and other no-iron fabrics.
- Before buying an item, scrunch a fistful of fabric, then see how it recovers. If it remains wrinkled, shop on.
- Keep washer and dryer loads small. Big loads mean big wrinkles.
- Use a cool-water rinse, and don't let the dryer get too hot. Heat sets in creases.

DRY CLEAN VERSUS DRY CLEAN ONLY

According to the makers of Woolite, there's a difference between a "Dry Clean" and a "Dry Clean Only" label. While "Dry Clean Only" usually indicates unwashable interfacing, lining, and covered buttons, "Dry Clean" signals a fragile fabric, but simple, washable construction.

If the label says "Dry Clean," place the item over a white paper towel and dab some cold-water wash on an inconspicuous spot. If the color doesn't bleed, save a few bucks and a trip to the cleaners by hand-washing it.

Dry-cleaning fluids are tough on fabrics, so whenever they can be avoided, the life of a garment is prolonged.

"I buried a lot of my ironing in the backyard."
—PHYLLIS DILLER

- Shorten the spin cycle. Spinning wrings wrinkles into clothes.
- Give wrinkle-prone items a good shake before they go in and come out of the dryer.
- Remove items from the dryer while they're still slightly damp. Shake, then hang till dry.
- If an item is still wrinkled, mist it with water and toss it back in with a damp towel and a new fabric-softener sheet. Tumble dry on low heat for a few minutes.
- Steam creased clothes in the bathroom while you shower, or buy a small plug-in steamer.
- Slip a wooden dowel through the hem of just-hung, slightly damp curtains to pull wrinkles out.
- If the weather is dry, put slipcovers back on furniture and throw pillows while they're still slightly damp. Not only will they dry wrinkle free, they'll shrink to fit.
- Fold two to four pieces of clothing within each other to puff out potential creases when packing a suitcase.
- Make wrinkles work for you. The more crumpled the shirt, the less wrinkled the face.

IRONING FOR FANATICS

If you absolutely must iron, here are a few ways to make it go faster and easier:

- Fill the iron with softened or distilled water to prevent clogging it with mineral deposits.
- Line the board under the cover with aluminum foil and run a warm iron over a fabric softener sheet for a smoother glide.
- Spray the board with water to dampen clothes.
- Spray clothes with warm rather than cold water to dampen them fast and evenly.
- Dampen and microwave heavy-duty wrinklers like linen and untreated cotton. Plop in a plastic bag and nuke on high for thirty seconds or so.
- Press only what shows: the collar and cuffs of a shirt worn under a sweater, the front of a blouse under a jacket, the bottom third of pants under a tunic.

"Why is there a permanent press setting on most irons"?

—KAY MOSURE

REIGNING CATS AND DOGS

You may have signed the papers and pocketed the key, but that unmistakable scent, chewed chair legs, and hair sprouting from the sofa mean only one thing—your home has been taken over by your pets.

Even though they protect us from vermin and varmints and love us no matter what, pets can also force us into a more intense relationship with our cleaning equipment than we're willing to commit to. But there are a number of ways to keep that relationship platonic.

CHOOSING A CLEAN BREED

Adopting a pet with a short, sleek coat is one way to go. Short-haired breeds like Chihuahuas and Abyssinian cats shed little, since they have little to shed; while Persian cats and sheepdogs can provide enough hair to carpet the house.

If Benji and Fluffy are already a part of the picture and look like they're going to stick around for a while, it's a good idea to get them used to spending more time outdoors.

THE GREAT OUTDOORS

There's no reason why a dog can't live contentedly outside, especially if he does so from the start, says dog trainer and animal behaviorist John Rubin. Dogs are generally more stimulated, happier, and healthier where they're free to run and soak up the sun and fresh air, he maintains. An outdoor dog is also less likely to shed year-round, since sunlight stimulates a natural yearly, or twice yearly, molt.

"The dog evolved outdoors," stresses Rubin. "It's what Mother Nature programed.

"A dog kept inside can become bored and destructive, since there are no new smells, sounds, and all the things they get outdoors."

An outside dog just needs to be hardy, and should have an enclosed yard or run and a soundly constructed pet house to keep him protected from the elements.

A good house should:
—be big enough to stretch and stand in, but small enough to be snug
—be built a few inches off the ground
—have a pitched or sloped roof
—be placed in a protected, tree- or screen-shaded area, faced out of the wind
—be close to the house, since that's where he most wants to be
—have soft, cushy, and washable bedding
—be well sealed and insulated against hot, cold, and wet weather (bubble pack makes a cheap, clean, and effective insulation)

Cats also do well outdoors. Our twelve-year-old, Frisky, has her own cat house, naps on the lawn furniture, prowls the perimeter of the house for mice, and uses trees, not table legs, to sharpen her claws.

> *"A dog will come when he's called. A cat will take a message and get back to you later."*
>
> —UNKNOWN

RESTRICTING

- If the outdoor life seems harsh, consider confining the pet to the laundry room, bathroom and/or kitchen where the floors are easy to clean and the upholstery is minimal.
- Install a pet door. Our neighbors have a set of pet

"I have always thought
of a dog lover as a
dog that was in love
with another dog."
—JAMES THURBER

doors leading from the laundry room to the garage, to a large fenced and tree-shaded yard. The setup gives their German shepherds independence, access, and shelter, yet it confines them to easily maintained areas of the house.

MAKING A HOME WITHIN A HOME

Crating a dog while it's in training or when you're gone for a few hours will prevent chewing and other destructive behavior. Dog trainer Brian Kilcommons says he wouldn't raise a puppy or train a dog without one.

"If the crate is used correctly, your dog will regard it as a room of his own," writes Kilcommons in *Good Owners, Great Dogs,* "Many anxious dogs actually enjoy being in a smaller, limited area, just like a little child might prefer to stay in his own room rather than wander around an empty mansion."

Trainer John Rubin agrees. "It's like a natural den to him. It gives a sense of security at home, on the road, or when he's injured or ill."

The best way to get a puppy or older dog used to a crate:

• Put him inside when he's tired and ready for a nap.

• Leave the door open, letting him come and go as he pleases, until he's used to it.

• Place his food and water inside, hooking up a gravity-fed water bottle to avoid spills.

• Line it with comfortable, washable bedding.

• Store toys and a few treats inside.

• Don't keep him confined for more than three or four waking hours

• Never use it as a jail when he misbehaves.

OFF THE FURNITURE

If they *have* taken over and you're too tired to teach an old pet new tricks, you can at least avoid furry furnishings by covering pieces with towels or washable blankets. A pet curls up in our favorite chair, not just because it's the best seat in the house, but because it has our scent. So snuggle into the cover for a few days till it's permeated to your pet's approval.

If you'd prefer not to share the furniture, keep a dog bed in the corner and a cat perch in a sunny window. A special pet cushion is nice, but a folded blanket, towel, or old rug will do the trick.

FURNITURE WARS

Sometimes we have to resort to weapons in the battle for furnishings.

A water pistol may work if you can catch the pet in the act. Some find vinegar is more effective than water, though one woman reported her dog actually liked being shot at and tried catching the stream in his mouth, vinegar or no vinegar.

Placing disposable aluminum baking pans on the edge of the kitchen counter or table can cure a curious cat of jumping up, and tying small inflated balloons low to chair and sofa cushions can have an even more startling effect.

Brian Kilcommons suggests booby-trapping a sofa or a chair with a few snap-type mousetraps set under a taped-down layer of newspapers.

"The traps will go off like little land mines when he climbs up, but because they're under the paper, he won't get pinched," he writes.

"But if you cuddle with him on the sofa, don't be upset when he sleeps there when you're gone," warns Kilcommons. "You can't have it both ways."

KEEPING A PET CLEAN

A cat does a good job of keeping itself clean, but a dog needs help. Frequent brushing is better than frequent vacuuming. Brushing also keeps odor under control and is good for his coat as well as his psyche.

A little baking soda or cornstarch rubbed into the dog's coat acts like a dry shampoo, but when he's really dirty or infested with fleas, you need to give him the dreaded bath. It's less messy to bathe him outside in warm weather, but when it's the middle of January and he just rolled in something the cat dragged home, he needs to get into the bathtub. Do it with less trauma to the dog, you, and your home:

• Brush first. If his coat is matted, spray it with a little cream rinse or conditioner.

• Smear a little petroleum jelly around his eyes and place cotton balls in his ears for protection against soap and water.

• Stuff a piece of steel wool in the drain. The ordinary rubber stopper that catches your tresses may not cut it with Rover's.

• Line the floor with beach towels or bath sheets.

• Keep the bathroom door shut. It will not only keep in the warmth but will prevent the dog from bounding through the house with a coat full of suds, should he escape.

• Leave his collar on, so you can keep a good grip. The leash isn't a bad idea either.

• Use a good pet shampoo or a mild human shampoo. But don't use too much of it. A rich lather is satisfying but hard to rinse off, and soap residue is irritating to his tender skin.

• Leave washing his head till last, since it's what he dreads the most. Besides, a good shake starts with the head, and a dog with a dry head is less apt to feel the need.

• Once he's thoroughly rinsed and squeezed, hold a big beach towel as a screen between you, the dog, and the rest of the room for the inevitable shimmy.

• Dry well with towels and a hair dryer before you open the door, since he'll probably run through the house like a maniac. For some reason a bath is as stimulating to a dog as a double espresso and a handful of chocolate-covered coffee beans to us.

DEALING WITH DOO-DOOS

Young, old, sick, and renegade pets are known to leave piles, puddles, and puke in remote corners as well as smack in the middle of the living room.

While distilled vinegar does a pretty good job of cleaning the offense, it's less effective as a deodorant. What's best is an odor neutralizer (found in most pet-supply stores) with a bacteria-eating enzyme. Whatever you do, don't use an ammonia-based cleaner. Ammonia only intensifies the smell of urine and attracts the pet to the same spot.

Even if there doesn't seem to be any stain or odor after picking up a dry stool, dab on a little neutralizer. A pet's sense of smell is much stronger than ours, and it is drawn to its old haunts. Also, damp weather can reactivate smells that seemed to be long gone.

Sometimes a wet stain goes through the carpet to the spongelike padding below. If it's very wet or widespread, you may have to rip up a portion of the carpet, cut out the damaged pad, and replace it. If it doesn't seem too extensive, fill a hypodermic needle with odor neutralizer and inject it through the carpet into the pad.

• Avoid all of the above by taking him to the groomer.

DECORATING GONE TO THE DOGS

• Color-coordinate the pets with the furnishings. A tweedy peach sofa and a Pekingese are good companions. A solid navy chair and a white angora cat are not.

• Avoid loosely woven fabrics like chenille and basket weaves. Tightly woven cloth like denim and gabardine are less vulnerable to sharp claws.

• Shun grass and rope rugs, since claws get caught in them.

• Avoid leather and vinyl. Once they're scratched and punctured, they're difficult, if not impossible, to repair.

• Use fabrics with good abrasion resistance to scratching. Nylon, acrylic, and polyester have it. Silk and acetate do not.

• Have an extra set of slipcovers on hand.
• Spray upholstery and drapery fabrics with a stain protector.
• Slip the comforter into a washable duvet if you like sleeping with furry, clawed creatures.
• Avoid a quilted bedcover, since the stitches are casily snagged in claws.

No More Dirty Dogs or Calamitous Cats

• Keep litter boxes off carpets and rugs, since pets sometimes miss, and fibers absorb odors.
• Place an absorbent mat under a pet dish to absorb spills.
• Provide a wide-mouthed bowl for a pug-faced dog like a boxer, and a narrow-mouthed, wide-bottomed bowl for a long-nosed, long-eared dog like a beagle, so the food doesn't get all over the dog and the floor.
• Prevent hairballs under the highboy by brushing a long-haired cat and adding a teaspoon of vegetable oil to its daily diet.
• Spread a decorative stone mulch or grind a liberal sprinkling of black pepper over the soil of a houseplant to discourage a cat from using it as a litter box.

Who Owns Whom?

You know your pet owns you when:
• *You buy more toys for the dog and/or cat than you do for the kids.*
• *You rent pet videos to keep your pet entertained.*
• *Your pet sleeps on down while you sleep on foam.*
• *There are hairballs in your pantyhose drawer.*
• *The groomer's bills are higher than your hairstylist's.*
• *Your pet's shrink is hostile to you.*

• Make sure a dog gets enough stress-relieving exercise. It'll make him less destructive and more mellow.

• Provide plenty of chew toys for a dog and a scratching post for a cat to distract them from furniture legs.

• Hard to fathom, but cat litter is a gourmet treat to some dogs. Keep it in the bathtub, so it's easy for Kitty to reach, but hard for less agile Rover.

Chapter 10

DIE-HARD HOUSEPLANTS

"A houseplant will never talk back to you, and you don't have to walk a begonia."

—LYNN RAPP

A few lush, healthy houseplants can bring a room to life or screen a mess, and may even clear the air of household pollution.

But rather than the fussy types that need more care than the kids, stick to the following diehards that are relatively unfazed by neglect:

THE HEAVYWEIGHT CHAMPIONS OF THE PLANT WORLD

• *Sansevieria or snake plant*   The toughest of the tough guys, sansevieria is a snakeskin-patterned succulent, with upright, sword-shaped leaves. It's a favorite among city dwellers, since it needs little light and is unfazed by pollution. If this can't take it, nothing will.

• *Cast-iron plant or aspidistra*   The Arnold Schwarzenegger of houseplants, with large, glossy leaves and rugged good looks. It seems to thrive in dark, forgotten corners, though it prefers filtered sun. It can often be found in the outdoor section of nurseries but makes the transition inside easily.

• *Chinese evergreen or aglaonema*   A hardy tropical plant with oval silver and green leaves. A real trouper, it adapts to conditions from hot and dry to cool and moist, but is happiest in bright light, where it puts forth lush, thick foliage and greenish-white flowers.

• *Dracaena*   This plucky plant comes in many varieties, but the most popular is a palm look-alike that can grow up to fifteen feet when it is happy, which is most of the time. It thrives in a wide variety of light conditions from full sun to deep shade, and likes to dry out between waterings.

• *Dieffenbachia*   A robust, upright plant with ivory and yellow streaked oval leaves. It likes filtered light and warm moist air, but will tolerate almost anything but over-watering.

• *Philodendron*   An almost foolproof climbing and trailing vine of nearly 300 varieties. It does as well in a bright, air-conditioned den as it does in a dimly lit, steamy bathroom. Just don't let its soil dry out.

• *Pothos*   Another sturdy climber and trailer, it has smooth green heart-shaped leaves splashed with yellow. It loves warmth and humidity, but tolerates cool, dry rooms and can go for long stretches without water. It also performs well under most lighting conditions except for direct sunlight and complete dark.

• *Cactus*   A member of the solid succulent family, it stows water in its sculptured body to withstand drought. There are hundreds of varieties of cacti, many with prickly spines and bright flowers. Its needs are few: bright sun and dry soil.

• *Kalanchoe*   A strong succulent with scalloped waxy leaves and clusters of red, pink, yellow, or other brightly colored flowers. It blooms up to three months and does well in filtered and full sunlight. It likes dry soil and infrequent, though thorough, watering.

• *Bromeliad*   A member of the pineapple family, it has gracefully curved foliage that forms a water-holding cup and a striking bloom that can last up to six months or more. It likes the light, and provided the pot is eight inches in diameter or larger, can go two weeks or longer without water.

• *Spider plant*   A green, or green-and-white burst that cascades in a profusion of parachutes. It thrives in a

"If it's raining in Arizona, water the cactus."

—OPAL'S ADVICE IN BRIAN CRANE'S *PICKLES*, A NATIONALLY SYNDICATED COMIC STRIP

warm, dry atmosphere and likes plenty of sun and water but will tolerate tougher conditions.

• **Kimberly Queen fern or Nephrolepis obliterata** Almost a dead ringer for the Boston fern, but it has none of its shedding and browning drawbacks. It prefers the light and likes moist soil and being pot-bound.

CHOOSING A HEALTHY PLANT

• Look for new growth, healthy color, and overall vigor, advises horticulturist and nursery manager Vickie Van Arsdale. "The bargain plants you see in places like supermarkets aren't always such a bargain," she said. "They're often grown too quickly in a hothouse and haven't been hardened off to normal temperature fluctuations."

• Detect hothouse wimps by their soft foliage and long stem growth between the leaves.

• Inspect joints and leaves for pests. A healthy plant won't have them, since pests usually go for a plant that's struggling.

• Avoid yellow, brown, and cracked leaves.

• Go for short and stocky, rather than tall and spindly.

• Look for strong, vigorous new growth. Buds are preferable to full-blown flowers, since it's fun to see them open and they'll last longer.

LOCATING

Even hardy types can wimp out if they're not provided with the basics. So here's how to make those tough guys even tougher:

• Find a comfortable spot. "Plants enjoy environments that people enjoy," says Van Arsdale. "They like it where it's bright, cheerful, and the air is good. With the exception of ferns, that like it cool, most plants like the same temperature as people."

• Read and retain the tag. Some plants are sun-bathers, while others prefer shade. A plant with deep-green leaves generally needs the least light, variegated leaves need a little more, and a flowering plant needs it brightest.

• Keep plants away from heating ducts, radiators, and fireplaces.

• Open a window in good weather. Plants love fresh air.

WATER BABIES

Even the brownest of thumbs have been known to turn green with hydroculture. And by growing plants in water, you avoid messy soil, repotting, and the worry you're over- or underwatering.

Some plants actually do better in water than in soil. The philodendron, for instance, often grows denser, darker leaves, and a dracaena can climb to great heights when its roots are submerged.

Other plant amphibians:

• *aspidistra*
• *Chinese evergreen*
• *dieffenbachia*
• *Hawaiian ti-plant*
• *pothos*
• *sansevieria*
• *Swedish ivy*

For best results:

• *Use glass containers: vases, bowls, and laboratory flasks. The latter can be found at chemical supply stores.*
• *Wash away soil and trim off any dead roots.*
• *Place a couple of inches of clear marbles, decorative stone, or aquarium gravel as a root anchor.*
• *Anchor the plant first, then add water.*
• *Drop a few charcoal chips in the water to keep it fresh.*
• *Place the container in a bright but not sunny spot.*
• *Feed once a month or so with a water-soluble plant food.*
• *Add water when needed.*

NATURE'S HOUSE CLEANERS

You can always go fake, but plastic and "silk" only gather dust, while the real thing counteracts dry air, increases oxygen, and may absorb household pollutants like formaldehyde and carbon monoxide.

Homes are full of gases that are emitted through carpeting, furniture, and cleaning products. According to the Environmental Protection Agency, the average house contains between 100 and 200 pollutants and is two to five times dirtier than the air outside.

But scientist Bill Wolverton, while working on reducing pollutants in space capsules for NASA, found that houseplants, including philodendrons, pothos, dracaena, sansevieria, and spider plants, absorb toxins through their leaves, roots, and soil, and recycle them into oxygen.

Some scientists are skeptical, saying there is not enough evidence to support these claims. Others say you'd need to live in a greenhouse to reap the benefits of these living cleaners.

While the jury is out, some horticulturists recommend using at least one twelve-inch potted plant for every 100 square feet, and cultivating a variety of plants, since certain species, it seems, prefer dining on particular pollutants.

• Divert curious cats by growing a pot of wheat or oat grass in a sunny window so they have their own plants to chew.

• Try a plant in various locations to see where it's happiest. Like real estate, location is everything.

WATERING

• Buy one of the above in at least an eight-inch pot and you can go up to two weeks without watering. (The exceptions are the spider plant and the Kimberly Queen Fern, which like more frequent watering.)

• Fill the watering can the night before so harmful chlorine and salts evaporate.

• Save the water from an aquarium or fishbowl when refilling. Houseplants love the nutrients in algae.

• Water when there's grayish soil and foliage, a light pot, and/or drooping leaves. Or try the old finger-in-the-soil test: if soil clings to your finger, hold off for a while. A clean finger means the plant needs water.

• Cover the drainage dish with a layer of pebbles or aquarium stone, so plants don't sit and rot their bottoms in a puddle should you overwater. The excess water under the stone also increases humidity around the plant.

• Always move plants to a waterproof surface before watering, in case of overflow.

• Plants look pretty spilling their leaves over ledges and shelves, but don't risk life and limb by watering them in high places.

FEEDING

Since plants leach nutrients each time they're watered, either use a timed-release fertilizer or add just a trace of conventional fertilizer with every watering.

POTTING

• Slip plants into something pretty. Plastic pots are nonporous, so they retain moisture better than clay, but plastic is, well, plastic. A plant looks better when it is placed, along with a drainage dish, in a decorative pot or basket.

• Double pot to increase the humidity and prolong time between waterings. Double potting also keeps the visible pot cleaner. Just make sure the decorative pot is large enough to provide needed air circulation.

DUST AND BUG BUSTING

• Spray. Dust is bad news for plants, since it prevents light from penetrating leaves effectively. And dusty plants tend to be more pest-prone. Spraying with water helps, but commercial leaf polishes are even more effective, accord-

"Have nothing in your house you do not know to be useful or believe to be beautiful."

—WILLIAM MORRIS

ing to Van Arsdale, since their oil residue discourages bugs from hatching.

• Use pump rather than aerosol polishes. Aerosols can freeze and damage leaves and are harmful to the environment.

• Make a natural insecticide with soap and water or by steeping chopped garlic and onion in water for a day or so. Spray plants every so often as a preventative measure.

DECORATING WITH HOUSEPLANTS

• Invest in a few large plants rather than a bunch of little ones. A larger plant makes a greater statement and requires fewer waterings.

• Buy a container to suit the plant as well as its surroundings. Mexican clay pots are compatible with cactus, succulents, and informal settings. Porcelain and brass fit formal plants and rooms, while baskets look right with most plants almost anywhere.

• Let the pot play up the plant, not dominate it.

• Cluster plants for humidity and effect. Arrange at least three together (odd numbers look best) and have shorter plants "step up" to taller ones on inverted pots.

• Backdrop low, bushy plants like kalanchoe or Chinese evergreen against tall, spiky plants like dieffenbachia or sansevieria.

• Use a baker's rack to mass and show off plants. The wire shelves seldom need to be dusted, especially if they have a mottled finish.

• Screen a habitually messy desk or corner with a row of tree-sized plants.

• Support a climbing plant against a graceful, pruned-to-scale tree branch. Tie with raffia or strips cut from a plastic bag.

• Use natural companions to set off plants: a bowl of goldfish, a collection of seashells and rocks, a piece of driftwood.

• Hang framed botanical prints nearby, or cluster

plants on a table covered in a floral or animal print fabric.

• Place a plant in front of a mirror to double its visual effect.

• Cast leafy shadows on the walls and ceiling by placing a small spotlight at the base of a large plant.

• Use moss (sold at most nurseries) at base of the plant to cover the soil, to hide the gap between the potted and decorative pot, and to hold in moisture.

• Protect tabletops and floors from moist pots by placing them on trivets, tiles, mirror rounds (found in bed and bath shops), or other nonporous barriers.

• Limit plastic and "silk" plants to hard-to-reach and hard-to-scrutinize shelves.

• Compost or chuck plants that have become sad and scraggly. Plants grown long in the tooth add nothing to the decor.

• Avoid the temptation to fill every empty corner with greenery. The jungle look went out with macramé and beaded curtains.

Chapter 11

REGIONAL
CHALLENGES

*"How ya gonna keep
'em down on the
farm?"*

Where we live often affects how much housework we have
to do.

A home next to a smoke-spewing factory or a dirt-
swirling farm is going to get a lot dirtier than one sitting on
a golf course or on the top of an air-conditioned high-rise.

Climate is also a factor. High humidity makes mold,
mildew, and rot a full-time hassle, while intense sunlight
and dryness wreak havoc on fabrics and furnishings. So
what works on the muddy shores of the Mississippi may
not cut it in the polluted air and concrete of Manhattan or
the dry desert air and sands of Scottsdale, Arizona.

SALTY AIR AND SANDY FEET

While there's a lot to be said for living by the ocean, keeping house isn't one of them. Corroding metals, mildewed
fabrics, and sandy floors are enough to make you want to
forget civilization and pitch a tent on the beach.

Registered nurse Louise Phillips thought she had
died and gone to heaven when she first moved to a beach
house on Maui. That is, until her silver service pitted, her
cast-iron pans rusted right in the drawer, and her carpets
crunched with sand. If you're part of the beach scene,
here's how to cope with the problems in paradise:

- Rig up an outdoor shower and set a footbath by the

door to desand beachgoers before they enter the inner sanctum.

• Have the kids wrap themselves in towels and slip out of sandy swimsuits before they come inside.

• Keep plenty of towels on hand and designate a sunny place to hang them.

• Install floor drains wherever possible, so sand and water can be easily swept and sucked away.

• Replace scratch-prone wood floors and sand-trapping carpet with tile, vinyl, or stone.

• Match the floor color as closely as possible to the color of the sand in the yard.

• Install low-glazed or slightly textured flooring so it's not slippery when wet. One savvy home owner installed gray pebbly stone tiles, each slightly convex, so sand sifts to the sand-colored grout.

• Lay an inlaid rather than a rotogravure vinyl floor. The latter has the color and pattern printed only on the top layer. Inlaid has multiple layers of granules fused into a durable, abrasion-resistant floor with a subtle sandy look that camouflages beautifully.

• Use steel-galvanized nails, fittings, and other hardware.

• Replace corrosion-prone metal furnishings, lamps, and accessories as they rust out, with stone, glass, and ceramics.

• Invest in rust-resistant enameled cookware.

• Mount plastic lenses on indoor and outdoor light fixtures.

• Paint, don't paper, walls. High humidity causes wallpaper to buckle and peel.

• Order noncorrosive steel chains on window blinds instead of rust- and pitting-prone aluminum.

• Ocean air causes paint on a wood exterior to blister and blow out to sea unless the prep work is meticulous. Painting contractor David Finlayson, who restores homes along the Massachusetts coastline, suggests caulking the

"People who live in glass houses have to wash their windows all the time."

—Art Buchwald

butt-edge of every board and seam, and using a top-quality high-gloss paint.

• Consider wrapping the whole house in low-maintenance vinyl siding.

• Make sure windows and doors are tightly sealed with weather-stripping to protect against sand dunes in the living room.

• Install copper window screens, flashing, railings, and rainspouts. They're expensive initially, but they weather well and turn a fashionable verdigris in the process.

IN A HILL, BY A BOG, OR SURROUNDED BY WOODS

While dampness is always a bugaboo at the beach, it can also be a problem with a home built into the side of a hill, in a low-lying area, or deep in the woods. Dampness brings on mold, mildew, and rot and increases a home's susceptibility to pests, so it's crucial to waterproof and ventilate.

• Make sure soil slopes away from the house for proper drainage.

• Extend downspouts so water drains at least three feet from the foundation.

• Clear clogged gutters so they don't overflow on exterior walls.

• Lay heavy (at least six-millimeter-thick) plastic sheeting over the soil in a crawl space, running it at least four inches up the walls.

• Seal absorbent masonry walls that abut a hillside.

• Install a sump pump to handle flooding.

• Cut back trees and bushes near windows to let in light and air.

• Make sure sprinklers don't hit the house siding.

• Consider installing a sun-catching skylight or two. Choose a raindrop-camouflaging milky or tinted type, and make sure it's convex or is set into a sloped roof so debris falls free.

• Shop for a vinyl floor with a built-in mildew-fighting barrier like Congoleum's "Bac Stop" or Armstrong's "Rearguard."

• Avoid wool carpeting. It's been known to smell like wet sheep when damp.

• Buy paint with a mildewcide additive, or have it mixed in at the paint store.

• Have vents cut into the peak of the roof and under the eaves on the windy side of the house to boost natural air flow.

• Encourage cross ventilation by opening windows that are placed diagonally across from one another. Windows directly opposite pull air from one to the other, but windows opened at an angle force air to circle around a room.

• Stir up the air with a ceiling fan. Run it in reverse to force warm air down along damp walls and windows.

• Install louvered doors in the pantry and on all closet doors.

PUTTING THE DAMPER ON MOISTURE

Wherever and whenever it's humid, consider the following measures to prevent mold, mildew, rust, and rot:

• Sprinkle moisture-absorbing cornstarch or talcum powder on mattresses when the sheets are changed.

• Choose synthetic fabrics over mold-attracting naturals.

• Hang rather than fold extra sheets.

• Don't store clothes in plastic dry cleaner or garment bags. Plastic encourages mold.

• Keep a low-wattage light burning in the closet, positioned at least a foot from clothes and cardboard storage boxes. If there's no outlet, consider mounting a battery-operated light.

• Check out plug-in electric rods used for drying things out on boats. One brand is called Golden Rod and is

---

THROUGH A GLASS DARKLY

In Southeast Asia, where humidity hangs heavy in the air, locals paint the backs of their mirrors with melted paraffin or beeswax to prevent the silver lining from deteriorating against damp walls.

---

available in lengths from 12 to 48 inches at boating-supply shops.

• Look into electric towel-warming rods, or use plastic or glass rods instead of corrosion-prone metal or rot-prone wood.

• Hang towels on wide bars rather than towel rings, so they dry out faster.

• Don't rely on an electric dehumidifier. It can dry out a room, but it needs to be drained and cleaned more often than it is worth.

• Use a moisture-absorbing chemical like silica gel or calcium chloride in closets and other enclosed spaces. Once it is saturated, dry it out in the oven or sun to use again.

• Give away the aquarium and keep houseplants to a minimum, since they boost humidity.

• Keep window coverings open to allow in sunlight.

• Never put away anything damp. Left to its own devices, a damp item can spawn enough mold and mildew to contaminate a drawer or a whole closet.

• Use plastic rather than wood, metal, and fabric hangers in closets.

• Install vinyl-coated wire shelves to promote air circulation.

• Add extra wall insulation to a closet with a chronic moisture problem.

• Store shoes, purses, and suitcases off the floor and on wire racks.

• Keep silver tightly wrapped in tarnishproof cloth.

• Use exhaust fans faithfully when boiling in the kitchen or bathing in the bathroom.

• Vent clothes dryers and exhaust fans outside, not into the attic, crawl space, or basement.

• Prevent cold-water pipes and air-conditioning ducts from sweating by covering their joints in waterproof duct tape and wrapping the rest in insulation.

• Wall-to-wall carpeting stretches and buckles in humidity, so have it restretched in summer rather than winter.

• Give furnishings time to adjust in a move from a dry to a humid climate. Wood absorbs moisture and swells, making doors and drawers stick.

OUTWITTING THE SUN

Intense sunlight can wreak havoc with fabrics and furnishings. So if you'd rather not spend your time and money replacing the draperies, carpets, and slipcovers every time you turn around, take heed:

• All fabrics, papers, and carpets fade in ultraviolet rays. Green turns yellow, black turns blue, and blue turns purple. Furnish with light tints and pale neutrals (heavily textured or patterned to foil soil) so fading will be less apparent.

• You might like exterior European-style roll shutters that operate from the inside. Not only are they effective sun blockers, but they give privacy and security, and negate the need for draperies and other window coverings.

• Consider factory-tinted windows and transparent solar shades. But don't apply solar film directly to windows. Nine times out of ten it bubbles, cracks, and peels. It's also been known to absorb enough heat to break glass.

• Shield skylights with shades, shutters, or sliding screens.

• Install canvas awnings over windows. Allow about an inch between the inside edge of the awning and the house, so hot air doesn't build up underneath. Awnings also protect a window from rain splatters and bird droppings.

• Plant deciduous trees to provide leafy cover in summer and bare-branch light in winter.
• Build a sun-filtering trellis over a south- or west-facing patio.

COUNTERACTING DRY AIR

Dry air, whether it's in Phoenix in summer or Fargo in winter, can warp wood, split leather, and cause carpets to snap, crackle, and shock.

A portable humidifier can dry out a room pretty efficiently, but like the dehumidifier, it can cause housekeeping problems. If the water supply is hard, white mineral dust is spewed over furnishings, floors, and electronic equipment, often causing the latter to malfunction. Even if the water is soft, it still needs to be changed and the reservoir cleaned frequently to prevent bacterial growth. Steam and warm-mist models are easier to maintain, since their filters remove minerals and their heat kills bacteria, but the hot parts and steam are dangerous around children, and they need changing and cleaning almost as often as a baby.

Better to keep the heat turned down and moisten the air with fresh flowers, a few large plants, an aquarium, or simply some pretty bowls of water. Other ideas:
• Use an antistatic pump spray on carpets.
• Mist wicker, cane, and rattan furnishings to keep them supple.
• Keep wood furnishings away from heating vents, wood-burning stoves, and frequently lit fireplaces.

SOIL ON THE MOVE

Whether you live on or near a farm, beach, or desert, the combination of wind and loose soil spell trouble. Dirt seeps through windows, cracks, and doors, and settles on everything in sight.
• Weather-strip windows and doors and caulk every crack, hole, and crevice.

- Plant, pave, and mulch the immediate yard, leaving no bare spots.
- Plant plenty of trees and bushes. Georgia Pacific figures that a large tree filters about 1,600 square yards of dust a season.
- Mandate a mud room, if you don't already have one. Screen off a section of a hallway, kitchen, or family room for removing muddy boots and shoes. Include a boot bin, brush, and shoe rack.

"Love your neighbor, but choose your neighborhood."
—LOUISE BEAL

INDUSTRIAL SOOT

Chances are, if you live in a city or close to a smokestack, you're fighting industrial fallout all through your home. Fight it by:
- Keeping windows and doors weather sealed
- Caulking all exterior cracks and crevices
- Using an air conditioner
- Decorating with muted colors. Bright, clear tones get dingy fast, while grayed or neutralized shades like Wedgwood blue, khaki, paprika, saffron, bronze, mauve, taupe, and pearl gray conceal beautifully.

LOCAL COLOR

Before you shop for new flooring, take a close look at the dirt around your home. It could range anywhere from pink sand to red Georgia clay to chocolate brown loam. If you

ANCIENT POLLUTION

While it seems industrial pollution is an evil of the modern world, scientists at the University of Umeå in Sweden say it's been with us thousands of years.

Recently discovered sedimentary deposits show ancient silver smelters spewed lead, sulfur, and other toxic dust into Greek and Roman cities, polluting their lakes and dirtying their homes.

match it to the floor color, you can put off sweeping, mopping, and vacuuming indefinitely.

Ranchers Liz and John Seibold were tired of battling the mud that surrounds them at least half of the year in their Flagstaff, Arizona, house. So they've covered the whole first floor in locally cut flagstone and saved the carpet for the second floor.

"Even upstairs I've used a mauvy brown, kind of the same color as the dirt around here," said Liz. "If you can't fight it, you might as well join it."

Chapter 12

THE LOWDOWN
ON LOWLIFE

Even if your house is squeaky clean, it's a Club Med for pests, where the air is warm, the food is free, and the drinks are on the house.

The natural response to finding them partying in your pantry and drinking under your sink is to nuke 'em with pesticide. Don't. Pests are known to build up a resistance to poisons and become stronger, while we seem to be developing more and more health problems.

Poisons also offer only temporary relief, so unless you take preventative measures, they'll be b-a-a-a-ck.

"Will you walk into my parlor,' said the Spider to the Fly."
—MARY HOWITT

GENERAL PREVENTION

• Make sure all weather-stripping and window and door screens fit snugly.
• Caulk all exterior and interior cracks and crevices around the house.
• Keep the crawl space and the space under the deck free of debris and well ventilated.
• Cover a dirt floor in the basement. It's a playground for pests.
• Store firewood outside, well away from the house, bringing in only what you need when you need it.
• Keep the compost pile at the far end of the yard.
• Avoid overwatering the yard, so creatures don't emerge and seek drier ground inside.

*"We hope when the
insects take over the
world, they'll
remember with
gratitude how we took
them along on all our
picnics."*

—BILL VAUGHAN

• Dispose of apple cores and the like only in the kitchen trash where it's more likely to be dumped daily.

• Tightly cover in-house garbage and compost scraps.

• Empty the refrigerator drip pan every so often, so that it doesn't become the local watering hole.

• Empty bags of pet food into tightly lidded containers.

• Don't let pet food sit in dishes overnight.

• Repackage grain-based foods in lidded plastic containers during hot weather.

ANTS

There's nothing worse than biting into a doughnut by dawn's early light and finding a trail of ants extending from your chin to the pantry.

Summer is high season for ants to move inside, but they'll come running anytime their nests are disturbed, their food and water supplies run low, and there's a good store of sweets and grease in the house.

It's hard to appreciate when they're swarming all over the counters, but ants do have a good side: they scare off termites, carry off the putrid offerings Kitty leaves, and eat the eggs and larvae of fleas, flies, and moths. So while you may not want to cultivate them, you don't want to annihilate them either. (As if you could.)

Prevention:

• Sprinkle a barrier of boric acid powder around the perimeter of the house. Boric acid is a white crystalline compound that's mild enough to be used as an antiseptic for humans but is lethal to bugs. Keep it dry for best results.

• Cut back branches that touch the house, since they make such handy ant bridges.

• Provide an outdoor water supply during dry weather (a shallow pan or a dripping hose).

- Plant mint around the foundation of the house. Ants and many other pests hate it.
- Moat pet bowls in shallow pans of soapy water. I use the lid of a plastic shoe-storage box.
- Dunk flowers from the garden in soapy water before they go into a vase. Many flowers lure ants for pollination, but peonies, chrysanthemums, and nasturtiums are regular brothels.
- Sprinkle a barrier of pepper or bay leaves around the edges of pantry shelves.
- Place a bay leaf or two in the flour, baking mix, and sugar bins.
- Keep the toothpaste capped.
- Keep cakes, cookies, syrups, even cough drops in the refrigerator or freezer during hot weather.

"Adam had 'em."
—"FLEAS," BY
OGDEN NASH

Treatment:
- Pour vinegar, boiling water, or hot candle wax down too close-for-comfort nests.
- Draw battle lines with scouring powder containing chlorine bleach.
- Zap ants with household cleaners like Fantastik, Windex, or white vinegar.
- Douse trails with baby powder. It chafes their bodies and absorbs the scent that marks the trail.
- Treat them to the following:

  ANT SURPRISE
  ½ cup granulated sugar
  ¼ cup honey
  ¼ cup dry yeast
  Mix. Place in bottle or jar caps. Results in fatal indigestion.

FLEAS

Fleas have been getting into our homes and under our skins since at least the beginning of recorded history.

In ancient Egypt, a designated slave was smeared

with blood or some other flea lure and made to stand as a human pest strip. In the Middle Ages, the flea, carried on its host, the rat, was responsible for spreading bubonic plague and wiping out a good chunk of the population of Europe. In eighteenth-century France, fleas were so prevalent at court, the well-dressed aristocrat carried an ornate, long-handled rod to slip into a bodice or under a wig and scratch away.

Today, the human flea is all but stamped out in the Western Hemisphere, so usually the only way to catch fleas is to have pets.

Fleas spend only a fraction of their time on pets. The rest of the time they're having sex under the sofa and laying eggs everywhere else. To break the cycle, it's important to treat the pet, the inside of the home, and the yard all at once. Hitting the carpets one day, the pets the next, and the garden last is useless, since fleas jump from one spot to the other before you even put away the weapons.

Treating the pet:
• Wash with a pet shampoo that contains insect-repelling pyrethrin, a derivative of chrysanthemum flowers.
• Boil a few fresh orange peels in a cup or two of water. Steep and cool, then sponge it onto the pet's skin. Scientists at the University of Georgia have found the oil in orange skins to be a powerful flea repellent. It smells good too.
• Massage diluted Avon's Skin-So-Soft on your pet's skin. It repels fleas and moisturizes the skin.
• If you have a pool, invite Rover in for a couple of laps. Fleas and ticks can't tolerate chlorine.
• Comb your pet frequently. He'll love the attention, it's good for his coat, and it discourages fleas and ticks. Use a fine-toothed flea comb and drop the little buggers into a bowl of warm, soapy water.
• Avoid flea collars. Most are toxic and only move fleas to the back of the bus.

• Use cedar-filled pillows for pet bedding and cover them with white towels so you can keep track of the fleas' comings and goings.

• Supplement Fido's and Fluffy's diet with brewer's yeast, garlic powder, kelp, and zinc. All make the skin unappetizing to fleas. A little vinegar in the pet's drinking water should help too.

• Rub brewer's yeast right into the pet's coat, or use a powder made with natural flea repellents like rosemary, eucalyptus, and citronella. Do it outside, so fleas flee into the yard and not into the home.

"Never use a hatchet to remove a fly from the forehead of a friend."

—CHINESE PROVERB

Treating the house:

• Sprinkle table salt or diatomaceous earth on carpets. Diatomaceous earth is a nontoxic fossil-shell dust that looks as fine as baby powder but cuts fleas to pieces. Use "garden grade," found in nurseries.

• The vacuum cleaner is a shuttle for fleas, ferrying them from room to room, so keep a few mothballs or a flea collar in the bag or destroy it after every use.

• Turn on the furnace occasionally in wet weather or when fleas are in high season. Fleas thrive where it's moist, and dry up where it's not.

Treating the yard:

• Sprinkle garden-grade diatomaceous earth around the yard, especially where pets hang out. Spread it around only on a windless day and wear a mask so you don't inhale it.

• Forget the TV for entertainment. Instead set up a:

FATAL FLEA CIRCUS
1 gooseneck lamp
1 floor
1 shallow bowl of warm soapy water
Place lamp on floor. Place bowl under lamp.
Watch the little suckers jump on the bulb, fall off, and drown.

COCKROACHES

Roaches may be the most repulsive of the lot. Like other creatures of the night, they love the dark and fear the light. And as they scurry through the house, they vomit and defecate, spreading disease-carrying germs.

They come into the home in the larvae stage on grocery bags, cartons, and sealed boxes of food, and once they get comfortable, they breed like crazy. One pair can produce thirty thousand offspring in a year, and for every one you see, there are probably a hundred more.

Roaches will eat everything from bad sauerkraut to good cigars, but they can also live without food, drink, and even their heads for three weeks. They can survive up to fifteen minutes under water and are immune to most poisons. So it pays to practice prevention, and if they do move in, make their lives so miserable they'll pack up and seek more hospitable quarters.

Prevention:
• Install air vents in the attic and promote good air flow throughout the house. According to USDA experiments, roaches hate breezes.
• Keep food tightly sealed.
• Thoroughly rinse food and drink containers before they go in the recycling bin.
• Repair leaky faucets and pipes.
• Never let dirty dishes sit overnight unless they're fully submerged in soapy water.
• Request plastic sacks at the supermarket, or better yet, provide your own reusable bags.

Treatment:
• Sprinkle boric acid around baseboards, under appliances and furniture, and in cracks and crevices.
• Set sticky traps like Roach Motels. Though they won't trap many roaches, they will indicate where they hang out for further action.

- Don't waste money on ultrasound devices. According to a USDA study, they don't work.
- Instead try:

   CHOKED ROACH
      4 tablespoons borax
      2 tablespoons flour
      2 tablespoons cocoa powder
      Mix well. Pour in jar covers. Place in suspected hideouts for a midnight snack with a whack.

SPIDERS

Spiders are good. Really. Their meal of choice is insects; in fact, they'll eat hundreds of flies, moths, and even roaches in a year.

Spiders spend hours refining their homes into such works of art, people replicate them. Tiffany often incorporated spiderweb patterns into his stained-glass lamps and panels. Members of the 1994 U.S. winter Olympic team had them designed into their Spider-Man bodysuits. Cher has a canopy like a silk web draped over the four-poster in her Manhattan apartment.

Spiders are good housekeepers, so if you see a dusty, sagging cobweb in the corner, chances are the owner has moved and it's safe to dismantle.

Of the hundreds of species, about the only spiders you have to be wary of are the black widow and the brown recluse.

The black widow, the "fat lady of the spider world" has a shiny body with a red or yellow hourglass design on the underside of its belly, and packs a powerful bite. It prefers dark, close-to-the-ground, out-of-the-way spaces, usually outdoors, so it doesn't normally choose an active household to set up shop.

The brown recluse is shy, but unlike the black widow, it prefers the indoors, especially enclosed spaces like attics, garages, and shoes. It has a yellowish-brown body, a violin-shaped mark on its back, and delivers a nasty but seldom fatal bite.

Treatment:

• If you must get rid of nonpoisonous spiders, carefully sweep them out the door where they'll benefit the garden or the neighborhood.

• Keep the yard, garage, and basement free of spider-hiding clutter and debris.

• Wear gloves, long pants, and a long-sleeved shirt to prevent bites when cleaning out likely hiding places.

RODENTS

For relatively small creatures, rodents do an enormous amount of damage. Since they're always teething, they have to gnaw constantly, so they'll chew on wood, plastic, and almost anything that doesn't chew on them first. They have a particular affinity for electrical cords and have been suspected of causing more than a few short-circuit fires. You know you have them when you see small, black bulletlike droppings, hear scratching in the walls, or smell something musty in the cabinets.

The first line of defense is a cat. Even if she's not a hunter, her scent alone may scare them off. Other precautions:

• Replace deteriorated screens over windows and ventilation openings.

• Seal exterior holes or gaps and cover pipes leading from the house with hardware cloth, since a mouse or rat can elongate its body and enter through a hole as narrow as a quarter inch.

• Cover floor drains with grates spaced no wider than a quarter inch.

• Keep a few mothballs under the plastic liner of the garbage pail.

• Thoroughly scrape and rinse dishes that sit in the dishwasher overnight or longer.

- Screen chimney tops. Roof rats have been known to play Santa.
- Cut back bushes and trees at least eighteen inches from the house.
- Rodents thrive in the cover of ivy, pyracantha, and bougainvillea, so make sure none of them grow on the house.
- Harvest fallen fruits and nuts from the floor of the garden.

Trapping:

Rat and mouse poisons are extemely dangerous around people and pets. Traps are a better bet.

- Wash hands before setting traps. Rodents are suspicious of human scent.
- Place traps next to walls, where mice and rats feel more secure.
- Forget cheese as a lure. It falls off, hardens quickly, and becomes unappetizing even to rodents. Peanut butter is the snack of choice.
- Or try the following:

PETRIFIED VERMIN

> *2 tablespoons cornstarch*
> *1 tablespoon plaster of Paris*
> *1 tablespoon powdered sugar*
> *Mix well. Set out in bottle caps, jar covers, or squares of foil. Look for swift and permanent hardening of the arteries.*

Chapter 13

CURING
HOUSITOSIS

"One's home should smell as beautiful as it looks."
—BARBARA M. OHRBACH, AUTHOR OF *THE SCENTED ROOM*

Have you smelled your home lately? Does it conjure up the fragrance of baking bread or yesterday's fish fry? If strangers dropped in, would they know you had a litter box, a wet Labrador, and a hamper full of running socks?

The sense of smell is powerful. Scientists say it's more sensitive than our sense of taste, and that our brains devote more space to smell than they do to vision.

Smell is the first thing we notice in someone else's home, and the last thing we're aware of in our own. Stale, musty odors can make a clean home smell grungy, while fresh, pleasant scents make a little dust and disarray seem less important.

Sure, there are plenty of deodorizing sprays that will mask Rover's romp in the compost pile, but the effect is short-lived and, instead of "freshening" the air, such sprays coat the nasal passages with a chemically scented oil. Better to seek out and clean up the source of odor, open the house to fresh air and sunshine, and use natural scents that last longer, are safer for the environment, and are more satisfying to the nose.

ALL THROUGH THE HOUSE

• Air the place regularly. It's best to halfway open a window on the breezy side of the house or apartment and fully open another diagonally across from it. The diagonal positioning forces air to swirl around the room and sweep out odors.

• Set out bowls of vinegar to absorb cigarette, cigar, and heavy cooking odors.

• If it smells good, bring it in. Flowers are fragrant, but pine boughs, eucalyptus, and many herbs are longer-lasting.

• Change furnace and air-conditioner filters regularly so bacteria doesn't smell up and contaminate the whole house.

• Cultivate fragrant houseplants. The blooms of freesia, narcissus, hyacinths, cattleya orchids, and miniature gardenias are often short-lived, but their sweet fragrance makes up for their early demise.

• When you get around to vacuuming, drop a couple of cinnamon sticks, a sachet, or a cologne-saturated cotton ball in the vacuum bag.

THE KITCHEN

• Remove food odors from cutting boards, utensils, and hands with a squeeze from a lemon or lime.

• Don't let garbage ferment in the disposal. Flush it away quickly.

• Pull out and rinse the accumulated goop off the bottom of the rubber disposal gasket every so often.

• Grind an occasional chopped lemon or lime in the disposal to keep it smelling sweet.

• Keep the drain odor free by running hot water through it every day.

• Line a trash compactor with newspaper to absorb liquid and odors.

• Rinse fish and pet food cans thoroughly before they go into the compactor or recycling bin.

• If the automatic dishwasher is used less than once a day, sprinkle baking soda on the bottom to keep it smelling fresh.

• Clear the air after broiling or baking fish by plac-

ESSENTIAL OIL

Essential oil is a highly concentrated essence of flowers, herbs, or spices used to make and refresh potpourri. It can be found where potpourri is sold, as well as in many health-food stores. It's stronger and longer-lasting than cologne and perfume, since there is no alcohol to evaporate, so a drop goes a long way.

Patti Upton, the founder of Aromatique, a decorative fragrance line, moistens cotton balls with her oils and places them in the vents throughout her house. She says her mother drops a cotton ball saturated with "Smell of the Rose" and drops it into a vase of roses to intensify the scent.

In her book The Scented Room, *Barbara M. Ohrbach suggests rubbing a little favorite oil into the inside of drawers and storage chests or on the underside of a sofa table. The scent is released slowly and subtly, often lasting months. Ohrbach also drops cinnamon or balsam oil into pinecones she keeps piled in a basket near the fire. "Then I burn the cones with the kindling," she writes. "And you can imagine the heavenly fragrance that produces."*

ing a cut lemon in the hot oven and leaving the door slightly ajar.

• Store fresh-cut cooking herbs in a glass or vase of water so they add their scent to the room.

• Pour a couple of tablespoons of vanilla and a quarter cup of water into a pie plate and set in a 300-degree oven. Turn off the oven and leave the door ajar and it'll smell as if you've been baking all day.

• Keep empty cookie tins smelling fresh by storing a few whole cloves inside.

• Store a ventilated box of baking soda or a piece or two of activated charcoal in the fridge to absorb food odors.

• Sprinkle a few bay leaves on pantry shelves for a natural pest repellent with a subtle herbal scent.

• Simmer a couple of tablespoons of pickling spice in two cups of water on a back burner.

• Pile a bowl high with lemons or tangerines on the table.

• Plant fragrant flowers and herbs in a window box so their fragrance wafts through the room on a warm day.

"There is nothing like an odor to stir memories."

—WILLIAM MCFEE

THE CLOSET

• Line a closet with cedar siding, or tie cedar shavings in a mesh bag and hang on an inside hook.
• Ferry smelly socks and sweaty shirts to the laundry room before their odor permeates the closet.
• Keep closet doors open occasionally or install louvered doors to promote air circulation.
• Line drawers with scented papers or cedar drawer liners.
• Slip cedar shoe trees in shoes and boots to keep them in sweet shape.
• Replace mothballs with fragrant cedar chips or blocks, or mix up the following sweet-smelling moth repellent:

> *1 handful each, more or less, dried lavender and*
> *   rosemary*
> *1 tablespoon dried cloves*
> *1 whole lemon peel, chopped and dried*
> *Spoon into cotton hankies, tie with ribbon, and*
> *   tuck into clothes pockets and closet corners.*

• Spray cotton balls with your favorite fragrance, let dry, and tuck them into closet corners, nooks, and shelves.

THE BATHROOM

• Freshen a smelly shower drain with a handful of baking soda followed by a vinegar chaser.
• Unwrap pungent soaps like Zest, Irish Spring, or Yardley's English Lavender and stash them in bathroom drawers or pile them in a basket. Not only will they scent the whole room, they'll harden and last longer.
• Keep a chunky scented candle and a small box of

"Smells are surer than sights and sounds to make your heart strings crack."

—RUDYARD KIPLING

matches on the back of the toilet to burn off natural odors.

THE BEDROOM

• Tuck a fabric-softener sheet between the mattress and box spring.
• Float a fresh gardenia or two in a glass bowl on the night table.
• Plant a bed of night-blooming jasmine, honeysuckle, roses, or spicy petunias outside the window.
• Banish dank drawers with dried lemon peels.
• Place a vaporizer ring around a lightbulb and drop in a little essential oil, oil of wintergreen, or bath oil. The heat will release the scent.
• Ban food from the kids' rooms. Soured milk and moldy pizza under the bed can stink up the whole house.

THE FIREPLACE

• Enhance the aroma of the wood you burn. Lay a few logs of pungent juniper, sweet-smelling citrus, or maple among more common woods.
• Tuck dried citrus peel, cinnamon sticks, pinecones, or hickory chips among the logs just before lighting.
• Dry the woody stalks of annual herbs to use as kindling. Lavender, sage, mint, and rosemary are especially fragrant.
• Burn a cluster of fat, pine-scented candles on the grate when it's too much trouble to build a fire.

PETS

• Neutralize Rover's odor between baths with a handful of baking soda brushed into his coat.
• Sprinkle coffee grounds or baking soda at the bottom of Kitty's box before filling it with litter.

THE POWER OF FRAGRANCE

People have been using scent to influence behavior since ancient times. Cleopatra beguiled Marc Antony on her cedar barge with its perfumed sails and incense-permeated throne. Hosts in ancient Rome who believed certain scents prevented drunkenness sprayed banquet guests with scented waters from silver pipes and sprinkled them with petals that drifted from the ceiling. Women in medieval times sewed fragrant, sleep-inducing herbs into "dream pillows" to cure insomnia.

While it all may sound like so much hocus-pocus, scientists at the Olfactory Research Fund in New York are working to dispel skepticism in their pursuit of the powers of scent. Their clinical and laboratory tests indicate that mace, nutmeg, and lavender oil reduce stress; peppermint and lily of the valley energize; and heliotropin enhances sleep.

While these findings may be more beneficial on the massage table than they are in the home, maybe a little of the right oil in the vaporizer will motivate the kids to pick up, or at least relax us to the point where a little clutter isn't critical.

• Neutralize gamy odors by sifting baking soda onto the carpet and letting it sit overnight.
• Fill a pet's bed pillow with cedar shavings to discourage fleas and absorb odors.
• Line the dog run with fragrant cedar shavings, eucalyptus leaves, or pine needles.

OUTSIDE

• Keep the compost pile covered with a layer of sand or dirt to eliminate odor and to break down scraps faster.
• Cultivate scented geraniums in the garden. Different varieties have nutmeg, ginger, coconut, and other unusual scented leaves that can be used in arrangements or dried into potpourri.
• Plant a fragrant flowering tree or bush by the front door so the scent drifts into the house with each visitor.
• Cultivate white and light-colored flowering plants,

since they generally have more fragrance than those with darker blossoms.

NOOKS AND CRANNIES

• Hang a net vegetable bag filled with charcoal on the wall of the basement, garage, or anyplace it gets musty. Charcoal absorbs moisture and stale odors.

• Wrap a few cinnamon sticks in cheesecloth and place in musty cupboards and drawers.

• Keep a fabric-softener sheet in an empty suitcase.

• Tuck bars and slivers of sweet-smelling soaps in dresser drawers, storage chests, and the linen closet.

• Uncap and place a just-emptied bottle of perfume or cologne in a dresser drawer.

• Tuck a fragrance card that comes with your department store bill into a purse.

• Deodorize a musty book by sprinkling the pages with talcum powder and sealing it in a plastic bag for a month or so.

• Store a piece of charcoal in the filing cabinet to keep papers from getting musty.

REVIVING POTPOURRI

When the bloom is off the potpourri, it can be refreshed a number of ways:

• Add new color by air-drying fresh petals, berries, and small, well-formed leaves. Or dry them in a slow oven, watching them carefully so they don't burn.

• Add dried fragrant herbs like mint, basil, and rosemary to an herbal blend.

• Add cinnamon sticks, whole cloves, and allspice to a spicy blend.

• Tap a drop or two of a good essential oil in a compatible scent into the mix and shake it in a plastic bag.

• Toss out the old and experiment with your own new blend. Patti Upton said she developed her popular

"The Smell of Christmas" by gathering gum balls, hickory nuts, and pinecones from the grounds of her Arkansas home. She then threw in a few cinnamon sticks and berries, and blended it all in a big wooden bowl with a few essential oils. "It just kind of happened by accident," said the owner of the now-multi-million-dollar decorative fragrance business.

Chapter 14

BEAT THE
BACKYARD BLUES

"A weed is a plant whose virtues have not yet been discovered."

—RALPH WALDO EMERSON

Dreams of a green lawn, drifts of flowers, and a house with curb appeal often turn to dust when we're confronted by the realities of lawn mowers, spades, and paintbrushes.

Yet it's possible to have a nice yard and a house the neighbors don't shun with less time in the bush and more in the hammock.

TWENTY STEPS TO A LOW-MAINTENANCE YARD

1. *Go native.* Scout the nearby countryside and check out the natives that need no artificial support system. Indigenous plants are available at most home and garden centers, and some nurseries specialize in them. Natives have a strong constitution, know how to shrug off disease and pests, and require little water and care once established. Cultivate them and you'll have nature on your side.

2. *Go natural.* Stick with the irregular, free-flowing shapes found in nature. Straight lines and geometric shapes require constant shearing and pruning, while natural, draping curves go with the flow.

3. *Copy.* Peek over the fence to see what grows well in your neighbors' yards. Then pick their brains to see what gives them the most success with the least work.

4. *Give it backbone.* Treat the yard as an outdoor

room. Use trees and shrubs as walls, placing them around the perimeter of the lot, then fill in with ground cover and a few long-blooming perennials. With such a strong framework, a few patches and weeds will hardly be noticed.

5. *Lose the lawn.* A lawn is thirsty, hungry, and needs more haircuts than a Marine recruit. Reduce or eliminate it altogether and replace it with a ground cover. Most ground covers need no mowing and take considerably less fertilizer and water than a lawn. They take time to fill in, but shallow rooted annuals such as alyssum or impatiens can be seeded among them, reducing weeds and adding temporary color.

6. *Borrow.* Frame a distant hill, the neighbor's flowering peach trees, or any desirable view so that it seems part of your landscape. The Japanese have long practiced this technique in their small, masterfully planned gardens.

7. *Accommodate.* If the ground doesn't drain well and stays wet, cultivate bog-loving plants. If it's dry and rocky, stick to plants that like it that way. Work with nature; don't fight it.

8. *Prepare the soil.* By turning the soil over, breaking it up, and adding amendments at a depth of about a foot at the onset, you will find garden work easier in the long run.

> *"Life is frittered away by detail. Simplify. Simplify."*
> —HENRY DAVID THOREAU

THE PRETENTIOUS LAWN

The lawn is a relative newcomer to the horticultural scene. Grass was used only as an accent to blooms, hedges, and gravel paths up until the nineteenth century, when England developed an affinity for wide swaths of manicured turf.

When American novelist Nathaniel Hawthorne visited the English countryside in the 1850s, he wrote home complaining about the artificiality and pretension of lawns, and longed to see again the yards full of wildflowers, nettles, and clover that were common in nineteenth-century America.

9. *Cover up.* Use decorative rock or stone to cover awkward patches where watering is difficult or where plants refuse to grow. Lay plastic first to keep down weeds.

10. *Cluster.* Mass a limited variety of plants in groups of three or more for effect and continuity. Massing has the added advantage that plants share the same food, water, and light.

11. *Look to the future.* Those cute little specimens in the nursery have a way of turning into towering monsters that overtake walkways, windows, and doorways, and need constant shearing and hacking. Read the tags and allow for the mature overall size.

12. *Cultivate succulents.* Succulents hoard water in their plump leaves during wet spells and slowly release it in drought. And their lush growth, rich textures, and often spectacular blooms beautify the garden without burdening the gardener.

13. *Go for the long haul.* Quick cover is alluring, but

SEVEN WAYS TO TAME A LAWN

If you can't live without a lawn, at least make it easier to maintain:
- *Replace hard-to-reach corners and isolated islands with ground cover or decorative stone.*
- *Outline it with edging: brick, railroad ties, or plastic molding to eliminate hand trimming.*
- *Get rid of trees in the middle of the lawn or encircle them with ground cover and edging.*
- *Water deeply and infrequently. Frequent, light sprinklings result in shallow, weak roots, weeds, and disease.*
- *Consider a manual mower. It cuts grass straighter than a power mower, so there's less water loss. It's also safer, so the kids can take over the job.*
- *Raise the mower blades to 2½ to 3 inches. Longer grass encourages deeper, stronger roots and provides moisture-holding shade in hot weather.*
- *Leave grass clippings where they lie. As long as they don't clump, clippings mulch and fertilize.*

HOW TO INTERVIEW A PROSPECTIVE PLANT

Ask these questions before you haul it home and promise to love, honor, and weed it:

- *How tall, thick, and messy will you be when you grow up?*
- *Are you going to block my walls and windows when they need painting?*
- *How much water and food do you need to stay healthy?*
- *Do you have or are you susceptible to communicable disease and pests?*
- *Do you have the habit of harboring rodents and other destructive creatures?*
- *Can you take freezing temperatures without cones and other ugly, protective clothing?*
- *Will you need stalking to keep you in line?*
- *Will you feel at home in my soil?*
- *Do your roots enjoy pushing up patios and driveways?*
- *Will you fend for yourself when I'm too tired to care, or will you sulk, dry up, and die?*

generally the faster a plant grows the more likely it is to have a short and messy life.

14. *Drip.* Install a drip system that waters at the turn of a timer. Deeper, slower, and less frequent watering encourages strong roots, drought resistance, and moisture conservation. And with drip's direct hit, fewer weeds take hold.

15. *Pot.* Flower and vegetable beds are labor intensive, but patio planters filled with flowers, herbs, and vegetables are practically weed free and bring plants up close where you want 'em. Hook them up to the automatic drip system and they'll practically care for themselves.

16. *Mulch.* Mulching conserves water, reduces weeds, and insulates plants. It also gives a professional, finished look to the yard. Use pine needles, cocoa husks, or cedar chips to add humus and nutrients to the soil.

17. *Extend paving.* Extending paving or decking adds extra living space and lessens garden chores. Slope it

AN EASIER MAINTAINED EXTERIOR

Painting the house is not one of the joys of home owning, but it can be avoided altogether by wrapping the whole thing in vinyl siding. Vinyl siding never needs painting, since the color goes all the way through, and it doesn't peel or pit. It's also resistant to termites and is easy to hose off. Plus, it comes in various clapboard widths, styles, textures, and colors.

Vinyl can also be painted, if you want to gild the lily. Just don't go to a darker shade, since it can absorb the sun's heat and eventually warp the vinyl.

Brick and stone are also maintenance free, but if you're stuck with conventional painted wood or stucco, here's how to make the paint job look better and last longer:

- *Prime the surface well.*
- *Use two coats of an acrylic-based paint.*
- *Buy the paint manufacturer's top-of-the line brand. Lesser qualities won't adhere and cover as well. Whoever said "You get what you pay for" had probably just used a cheap can of paint.*
- *Choose shades that age well: cream, gray, brown, and other muted, earthy tones. Bright, clear colors like yellow and pink quickly show wear and tear and fade fast in strong sunlight.*
- *Take into account that mid-toned and dark colors appear deeper on a house than they do on a color chip, and light colors appear paler.*
- *Realize dark and middle tones also look darker on a textured surface because of inherent shadows.*
- *Use a matte finish on the body of the house to minimize knots, holes, and other flaws, and a glossy finish around windows and doors to shed dirt.*

slightly away from the house for drainage. Add shade and comfortable furnishings and you'll take the pressure off inside maintenance.

18. *Give it focus.* Instead of more plants, use no-maintenance statuary, boulders, and stone benches to add texture and form and, with the latter, usefulness.

19. *Zone.* Designate an area to the side of the house for trash, recycling, storage, and composting.

20. *Eliminate.* Rip out and compost anything that

isn't providing shade, color, or privacy. Chuck it also if it's pest ridden or makes a general mess of itself by shedding debris on the patio or in the pool. Every plant should earn its keep.

"The soil conditioner still unmatched is a simple spade with a spouse attached."

—UNKNOWN

PREVENTING POOL PROBLEMS

People often spend more time slaving over their pools than they do swimming in them. If you have one, there are a few ways to make it less of a hassle:

• Remove perimeter plants that continually drop leaves, pods, fruits, and flowers. A big annual drop from an oak is preferable to the continuous drop from a pine.

• Build a pergola for debris-free shade, or buy a giant patio umbrella.

• Cover the pool to keep litter out and heat in.

• Position the sandbox far from the pool.

• Keep a small wading pool nearby to decontaminate the kids before they dive in.

• Invest in an automatic pool sweep with a built-in debris basket.

• Buy an automatic chlorine dispenser.

• Install a backwash valve for easier filter cleaning.

• Provide plenty of hooks outside so the sun can dry wet towels and swimsuits.

A SHORTER PATH TO OUTSIDE MAINTENANCE

• Use a garden hose to initially outline beds, borders, and paths in natural, sweeping arcs.

• Plant a shade-loving ground cover beneath trees to absorb leaves and other plant droppings. Those droppings in turn will break down and fertilize the ground cover.

• Don't plant trees or bushes close to a septic tank. Their roots may choke things up.

• Plant a window box of herbs outside a kitchen window for easy access when cooking.

*"A perfect summer day
is when the sun is
shining, the breeze is
blowing, the birds are
singing, and the lawn
mower is broken."*

—JAMES DENT

• Tape or paint the handles of small gardening tools in bright fluorescent colors so you won't lose them among the cabbages.

• Toss dirty all-weather cushions in the pool for an hour or so, then hose them off. The chlorine will loosen embedded dirt.

• Spray the barbecue grill with vegetable oil before firing it up for nonstick cooking and easy cleaning.

• Store outdoor toys in a lidded trash can: a short one for preschoolers, a taller one for older kids.

• Invert a child's wading pool over the sandbox to protect it from cat and other animal droppings.

Part III

ROOMS

Chapter 15

THE SELF-CLEANING KITCHEN

In the new millennium, perhaps the kitchen will be designed like the dishwasher, so at the end of the day we can close the door, push a button, and wake up to a squeaky-clean room.

Until then, here's how to make cleaning the hardest room in the house look easy.

BUBBLE, BOIL, TOIL, AND TROUBLE

- Grease coats and clings to every exposed surface in the kitchen, so replace frying and roasting with cleaner and healthier methods like steaming, microwaving, and outdoor grilling.
- Develop an intimate relationship with your exhaust fan. A fan pulls out grease and smoke before they pollute the place.
- Use covers and steam screens to contain splatters when cooking.
- Place a spoon rest next to the cooktop to keep counters gunk free when you are stirring soups and sauces.
- Fill casseroles only three-quarters full to prevent oven spillovers.
- Forget the killer-to-clean broiler pan. Wrap a pizza pan or cookie sheet with foil and broil chicken, fish, or whatever on a cake-cooling rack.

"Cleanliness is not next to godliness. It isn't even in the same neighborhood. No one has ever gotten a religious experience out of removing burned–on cheese from the grill of the toaster oven."

—ERMA BOMBECK

"Cleanliness is next to impossible."
—PORTABLE LIFE 101

• Clean as you go when throwing together a meal, to avoid facing a mountain of grungy pots and cemented puddles of gravy after dinner.

• Mobile grazing generates crumbs and spills, so make it a rule that food is only to be eaten at the table or counter, and he who eats it, cleans it up.

OUT OF SIGHT, OUT OF GRIME

A counter filled with equipment not only adds to the visual jumble but also to the time spent cleaning. An equipment-free counter is not only easier to keep clean, it *looks* cleaner when it isn't.

• Keep only the things you use daily on the counter: toaster, can opener, and coffeemaker.

• Protect small appliances from splatters by parking them in an appliance garage: a closed-off space between the counter and upper cabinet that gives a kitchen a streamlined look.

• Store spoons, whisks, and spatulas in a drawer, or hang them from a rack inside a cabinet door.

• Make the most of cabinet and drawer space with cup hooks, plate stackers, and drawer dividers.

• Food canisters get grungy and are a pain to clean around; move them to the pantry or food cabinet.

• Choose cabinets instead of open shelves, since shelves call for ordered arrangements and expose items to dust and grease.

• Chuck the superfluous. Cooking styles change, so the hot-dog cooker, fondue pot, and *The Joy of Aerosol Cheese* may not be as indispensable as they once seemed.

• Think twice before buying another "convenience." In an episode of Cathy Guisewite's comic strip *Cathy*, the kitchen equipment of the fifties shows: pan, spoon, and knife. Out of it came a typical Sunday dinner of roast chicken, mashed potatoes and gravy, stuffing, salad, two vegetables, homemade rolls, and an apple pie. It then shows the standard equipment of the nineties: food processor, bread maker, pasta maker, juicer, rice steamer, laser-cut European knife system, twenty-piece cookware set, etc. The typical Sunday dinner of the nineties? Microwave pizza.

WITHIN EASY REACH

• Keep tableware within an arm's reach of the dishwasher and/or table.

• Set aside a low shelf or drawer for the kids so they can reach their own food items. Professional organizer Mary La Flame reserves the bottom shelf of her pantry for peanut butter, boxed juice, sandwich bags, and such so her four kids can pack their own school lunches.

• Store everyday things in cabinets and drawers between knee and neck level, the "sometimes-stuff" in the highest and lowest shelves, and the "hardly ever" in the outer reaches of the basement, garage, or attic.

• Install vertical dividers in the cabinet nearest the oven to corral that rattling pile of cookie sheets, cake racks, and baking pans.

• Use lazy Susans in cabinets so all items are accessible.

• Fit the insides of cabinet doors with shallow wire racks for small, easily lost items.

• Saw a hard-to-reach shelf to half its depth so you can see and reach high items more easily.

• Install a three-inch-deep ledge between shelves for an easy-to-see, hard-to-lose row of frequently used canned goods.

MORE SMART STORAGE

• Slip bags of chips, rice cakes, and other "spillers" into clear canisters or sealed plastic bags so they don't spread themselves around the pantry.

• Store canned goods with the labels facing forward, so you can see what you've got at a glance.

• Keep a measuring cup in the rice, flour, and sugar for spill-free convenience.
• Round up coffee-brewing items: beans, grinder, filters, and scoop in a basket.
• Group pantry foods by category: baking supplies, condiments, cereals, etc., on separate labeled shelves.
• Have at least one deep drawer for pots and pans. It's hard to lose a pot and its cover in a drawer.
• Use see-through storage containers for easy identification; food is often forgotten in opaque containers until whiskers and worse have grown.
• Save search time by assigning specific foods to certain refrigerator shelves, including one for leftovers.
• Store meats on the bottom shelf of the refrigerator so juice won't drip down on shelves and food.

COUNTER CULTURE

Counters can be kept lookin' good when we consider the material.
• Plastic laminate is thin-skinned, so chuck the scouring powder in favor of a squirt of glass cleaner or white vinegar.
• If a counter isn't burnproof and knifeproof (like laminate), keep a trivet and cutting board handy for hot pots and sharp knives.
• When shopping for new laminate, steer clear of a hard-to-clean matte finish. Go instead for smooth, mid-toned, and patterned.
• Grout is a stain sucker, so apply a grout sealer on a tile counter every few months.

MINIMAL MAINTENANCE

• Keep refrigerator magnets, messages, and what-have-you to a minimum.
• Use the insides of cabinet doors for clippings, frequently used recipes, and phone numbers.

THE PERFECT KITCHEN COUNTER

While there's a wealth of countertop materials on the market, unfortunately none are without drawbacks. Plastic laminate burns, tile has stain-sucking grout, stone is porous, and quartz composite is hard on tumbling dishes and glassware.

Solid-surface counters, however, come close to perfection. Known under such trade names as Corian, Avonite, and Fountainhead, they're made of either acrylic or polyester composites. They're nonporous, so stains wipe up easily, and there are no seams, sink rims, or grout to grab gunk.

Houston kitchen designer and American Homestyle *correspondent Gay Fly likes a solid-surface material around sink and food preparation areas because it's easy to clean and relatively gentle on glassware. But because a solid surface is subject to burns, she specifies tile or stainless steel near the oven and cooktop areas.*

"There isn't a counter that can do it all," says Fly. "So I always specify a combination of materials."

• Instead of wallpapering the fridge with children's artwork, slip their masterpieces into clear plastic place mats designed for the purpose. First-grade teacher Nancy Shen has her students make their own place mats by laminating their artwork between clear adhesive paper and cardboard backing.

• Replace shiny cooktop drip pans with spill-hiding black models.

• Avoid scrubbing drip pans altogether by slipping precut aluminum liners over them.

• Run a greasy cooktop filter through the dishwasher.

• Easy-clean a microwave by nuking a couple of tablespoons of baking soda in a cup of water and wipe up the fallout with a paper towel.

• Line the bottom of the oven with aluminum foil.

• Blast away mineral deposits and keep the repairman at bay by pouring a gallon of cheap white vinegar in

"The best way to clean a frying pan that has burned food cemented to the bottom is to let it soak in soapy water for several days and then, when nobody is looking, throw it in the garbage."

—DAVE BARRY

the dishwasher every so often and running it through its regular cycle.

• Avoid hazardous and mostly ineffective drain cleaners by pouring a kettle of boiling water down the drains every week to keep them clear.

• Keep garbage disposal blades sharp by feeding them an occasional tray of ice cubes. Ice also dislodges tenacious bits of food.

• Save yourself the hassle of major refrigerator cleaning by wiping down a shelf or two when supplies run low.

• When remodeling a kitchen, choose ready-made cabinets with a catalyzed conversion varnish. Because this varnish can only be applied in a specially designed vacuum chamber, EPA standards prevent custom cabinetmakers and do-it-yourselfers from using this amazingly impervious finish.

REPLACING APPLIANCES

• Buy the most streamlined, knob- and gadget-free appliances you can find, since a mass of controls only means more bumps and crevices to clean.

• Avoid glass doors on all appliances, especially the fridge; not only do you have to clean the door frequently, but the insides are under constant scrutiny.

• Buy a fridge with glass shelves, since glass contains spills to one level and is easier to clean than wire.

• Nix options like ice makers and water dispensers, since they need twice the number of repairs of conventional refrigerators and frequently spew their contents all over the floor.

• Check out ceramic cooktops; their seamless and hole-free design makes for easy cleanup.

WALLS

The three kitchen walls easiest to maintain are tile, canvas-backed vinyl, and paint. Tile is stain repellent, and grout on a vertical surface seldom causes the problem it does on a counter or floor. Semigloss or satin-finish paint wears well, repels moisture, and cleans fairly easily. A canvas-backed vinyl wall covering cleans easily and with enough pattern and color can hide everything from tossed salad to flying oatmeal.

Some points:
 • Keep grass cloth, flocked papers, brick, and barn siding out of the kitchen. Once they absorb grease, they're almost impossible to clean.
 • Ban mirrored surfaces as well, since they need constant maintenance.
 • Protect a nonvinyl wall covering behind the cooktop with a sheet of clear acrylic, or protect a room full of it with a coat of polyurethane. Try the polyurethane in an inconspicuous spot first, since it has a tendency to yellow surfaces.
 • Install countertop material all the way up to the

THE BEST FLOOR

Tile and wood are popular choices in today's kitchens, but water and wood are seldom a good mix, and tile has crumb-catching, stain-holding grout.

A top-of-the-line no-wax sheet vinyl is best for low maintenance because the factory finish is thicker, maintains Peggy Lewis, an interior designer who specializes in floors.

Lewis said people often wear out that finish with harsh cleaners that leave a dirt-catching residue. She recommends testing a cleaner by applying it to a window and letting it dry. "If it clouds the glass, it's doing the same to your floors," she says.

She advises using the floor manufacturer's cleaner, or a weak solution of glass cleaner, vinegar, or ammonia in water. None need rinsing.

As with most surfaces in the kitchen, a vinyl floor with a low-gloss finish will help camouflage scuffs and scratches. And if it comes in a colorful splatter pattern, it can even hide the results of a food fight.

wall-hung cabinets, since this area is highly vulnerable to stains.

• Use a simple decorative paint technique like sponging, stippling, or splattering to give walls pizazz and conceal inevitable stains. Finish with a water-based sealer.

• Instead of trying to scrub a grungy ceiling, paint it a different but harmonizing color from the walls, since kitchen ceilings darken faster than walls.

• Store a tiny jar of paint along with a small paintbrush in a cabinet for quick wall touch-ups.

• Use a top-of-the-line paint; anything less may lack adhesion and washability.

FABRICS AND FURNITURE

• Hang either a simple vinyl-coated shade at the window or a no-iron cafe curtain that can be hung straight out of the dryer.

• Make sure all window coverings are a safe distance from the cooktop.

• Slipcover kitchen chairs and stools in machine-washable soil-hiding prints or upholster them in vinyl. Today's vinyls are more comfortable and less likely to crack than the old stuff and can be kept clean with a quick flick of the sponge.

• Cover an old table with ceramic tile for a heat-proof, stainproof surface that's easy to clean. Use machine-made tiles, since they provide a more even surface than handmade ones.

MORE GOOD CLEAN THOUGHTS

• Make an effort to eat together as a family. It will not only make for stronger bonding but will keep the kitchen and eating area cleaner.

• Pitch that slimy bar of soap for a decorative hand pump filled with dish detergent. Choose an opaque container to mask handprints.

• Use glass cleaner or vinegar to keep windows, counters, furnishings, and even most fabrics clean. Spot-clean spills to put off scrubbing.

• Avoid sticky pantry shelves by setting honey, syrups, and other "slow drippers" on small plates or flat plastic covers.

• Line the cabinet under the sink with leftover vinyl flooring.

• Sweeten a smelly garbage disposal by running lemon or lime peels through it occasionally.

• Get in the habit of immediately closing cabinet doors for a neater look.

• Apply a coat of polyurethane to keep cabinet shelves from blistering under damp dishes and to avoid the hassle of shelf paper.

• Avoid the need to scrub sediment from the coffeemaker by brewing coffee with distilled water.

• Cut down on dishwashing by cooking in containers that can go from the oven to the table to the fridge.

• Always place one cup upright in the dishwasher to tell whether the machine has gone through its cycle or not.

• Master the microwave; foods like scrambled eggs, sauces, and vegetables can be cooked in their own serving dishes.

• Invest in a couple of cast-iron pans. They turn black naturally, so scratches, stains, and dings don't show. They also add a nutritional dose of iron to foods.

• Instead of trying to scrub the hard-to-clean blender, whip up a soap-and-water shake.

• Don't waste time scrubbing burned pots and pans; just let them soak in a little vinegar and water.

• Replace grungy pot holders, sponges, and dish towels often. They're usually the most frequently overlooked items in a kitchen, but they make a difference in the overall picture.

• Hang the dish towel out of sight rather than on the refrigerator or oven door.

• Load forks, spoons, and knives in their own slots

in the dishwasher basket so you can quickly grab and put away a handful.

• Use personalized family cups and glasses to cut down on dishwashing. You'll also know who the culprit is when you find one where it doesn't belong.

Chapter 16

THE
DINING ROOM

Few of us can resist a formal dining room where the silver glitters, the linen dazzles, and the mahogany glows in the warmth of candlelight.

The trouble is, all that formality makes the room such a fuss to use, it sits alone much of the time looking like it's waiting for the butler to show up.

It's time we bring the room into reality.

"You can keep the dining room clean by eating in the kitchen."
—P. J. O'ROURKE,
THE BACHELOR HOME COMPANION: A PRACTICAL GUIDE TO KEEPING HOUSE LIKE A PIG

MAKING IT VERSATILE

Rather than let it gather dust between holiday dinners, consider using the room day-to-day for other purposes. The trick is to make the space flexible enough so it can swing in either direction. If furnishings are versatile and easy to move, it's fairly easy to convert the room back to its original purpose when the occasion arises.

• If the children are young, there probably isn't much time or energy for formal dining, so consider converting the space to a playroom for a few years. After a favorite tureen was broken, Bill and Cathy Hanlon took the long view and packed away the wedding gifts until their three young sons get older. They now store toys in the hutch and books on the shelves that will someday hold china and crystal again.

• Use the room as a study. The table provides a big

enough surface to spread out homework, correspondence, and bills.

• Find a chandelier with a down-light to illuminate projects as well as the porcelain. A dimmer switch can turn it up for close work and down for atmospheric dining.

• Line the walls with bookshelves to hold dinnerware and books. Under the shelves, add deep cabinets whose tops can be used as buffet space.

• Hide table clutter with a decorative hinged screen.

• Protect the table from homework graffiti, drinking-glass rings, and warm serving dishes with a coat or two of polyurethane. This Rambo-tough finish is resistant to marring, moisture, and to some extent, heat. It's easy to apply, requires no wax or polish, and is widely available at home centers and paint and hardware stores in matte and gloss finishes.

• Choose a matte polyurethane finish to better camouflage fingerprints and dust.

• Be aware that polyurethane can darken or yellow a surface somewhat. It also mellows it and gives it an antique look.

TABLE SHOPPING

• Search out a distressed table that already has the character and patina of wear. Old library tables are especially durable, and you don't have to treat them with kid gloves.

• Choose a table made of rock-hard oak or maple rather than one made with a softer, easily scratched soft wood like pine.

• Avoid dual surfaces. Marble or glass bordered by wood, for example, complicates the maintenance.

• Think twice about a glass top. Moisture doesn't faze it, but it scratches easily and shows every dust mote, smudge, and fingerprint.

• If you must have glass, choose a green, bronze, or gray tint to better camouflage the inevitable.

• If there's room, consider buying two same-size rectangular or square tables. Separate, they can be used for a buffet and small dining table. Together, they can seat a crowd.

• Choose a table with integral leaves, which are easier than loose leaves to set up and there's no storage problem. If leaves are separate, store them behind a towel rack screwed into a nearby closet wall.

• Seek out a table with a built-in drawer or two for convenient storage of flatware and place mats.

CHAIRS

• Buy chairs that have easily removable seat cushions, are light enough to move, and are stylish enough to be used in any room.

• Choose chairs with clean lines and a minimum of detail. Heavy, ornate carving gathers dust and takes time and effort to keep clean.

• Brush on a coat of polyurethane for a slick, easy-to-wipe, tough-to-damage finish.

FABRICS

• Limit upholstery to the chair seat. Food and fabric are seldom compatible.

• Cover seats with soil-repelling fabrics such as leatherlike vinyl or tapestry, which camouflages stains well. If cushions are tie-on, use a fabric that will come clean in the wash.

• Spray with a fabric protector like Scotchgard.

• Protect fabric from major mishaps by covering cushions with small towels when children are at the table.

SIDEBOARDS

• A good-sized sideboard or buffet can save trips to the kitchen and make serving meals more convenient.

Since it holds food and drink, it needs to be to be heat- and moistureproof. Paint it with polyurethane, or better yet, top it with tile, a custom-cut piece of Corian, or, if it's sturdy enough, a slab of granite.

• Choose a sideboard with a base that sits flat on the floor over a leggy model that traps dust underneath.

• If space is tight, hinge a drop-down serving shelf to the wall. Match it to the wall color, or stencil a design on its underside, and protect it with a coat of polyurethane.

STORAGE

• Store items where you use them. Table linens are better kept in a drawer or cabinet in the dining room, for example, than off in the linen closet.

• Store glassware and cups upside down to prevent dust and to discourage spiders and other critters from taking up residence.

• If drawer space is minimal, mount a spring-loaded clip on the inside of a cabinet door to hang place mats.

WALLS AND DOORS

• If the dining area is open to the kitchen, use a folding screen to hide the chaos of the food preparation area. A screen also blocks drafts and makes the space seem more intimate.

• Consider cutting a pass-through in the wall for easier access to the kitchen. Close it off with hinged shutters when it is not in use.

• Install a swinging door with a kick plate between the kitchen and dining room.

• Paint walls a deep, rich color for a warm dramatic background and to disguise smudges and wear.

• Hide chair scrapes with wainscoting. Apply heavily grained wood paneling, tile, or densely patterned vinyl wall covering about three feet up the wall. Cap with a chair rail.

A GOOD EXCUSE NOT TO POLISH

Grandma used to give her table a fresh coat of wax and a good dose of elbow grease once or twice a year to protect it and make it gleam. Today, a few diehards still follow this routine, but most of us spray on a coat of something or other regularly to attack dust and bring up the shine.

But according to Consumer Reports, *we're wasting our time. The publication reports that since most furniture (with the exception of teak) made since World War I is sealed with nonpenetrable lacquer, those oils, waxes, and sprays don't do much good and can actually attract dust and magnify fingerprints.*

We're better off wiping with a plain water-dampened rag or, if the surface is really grungy, a rag moistened with diluted all-purpose cleaner.

Just remember, too much of a good thing can hurt. When the rag is sopping with water or cleaner, the lacquer can blister and crack. Better to spare the rag and save the table.

• Go Shaker style and install a row of sturdy pegs around the room to hang chairs for easier floor cleaning.

THE MAGIC CARPET

I once had a house with white wall-to-wall carpeting throughout, two kids under three, and an urge to host every holiday, birthday, and special-occasion dinner that came our way. It wasn't long before the carpet under the dining table looked like a pizza with the works, so to protect it from further abuse, I covered it with a big, cheap cotton rug in a tight Persian design colored in food tones of deep red, green, tan, and ivory. Spaghetti sauce, spinach, gravy, ice cream, you name it, eventually landed on the rug, but they all magically blended into the design.

The kids are grown and the old rug has since been replaced, but I'll never be without the king of camouflage under the table—an Oriental rug.

• Whether you are buying a traditional Oriental or a contemporary-design rug, choose one with a dense pattern and mostly deep shades (and a few light tones to disguise lint) instead of a rug with a large plain field in pastel tints.

• Stick with solid or striped walls and fabric patterns that are markedly larger or smaller in scale to complement the rug's strong design.

• Lay a rug that's at least two feet wider and longer than the table, so chair legs won't catch in its edges. If your table is four by six feet, for example, the rug should be at least six by eight.

• Place padding under the rug to make it last longer and feel plusher.

• Turn the rug periodically so it will wear evenly.

• Stick with a low, dense, level loop pile. Shaggy rugs do not belong under falling food.

• Stash a small terry towel behind a cabinet door so there's no panic when a spill occurs.

• Blot up food and drink stains promptly, but don't mess with mud. If some ogre stomps across your rug in muddy shoes, let it dry, then brush it off.

• Save the manufacturer's label from a new rug, in case any questions arise regarding care or warranty.

• Avoid a sisal, coir, jute, or sea-grass rug under the table. Such materials stain easily, snag under chairs, and are difficult to clean.

• If you like bare wood floors, paint or stencil a rug to visually anchor the table and camouflage spills.

LIGHTING

• Create a pool of light over the table. In *A Pattern Language,* a book about the psychological effects of our surroundings, architect Christopher Alexander and his associates advise against even, all-over lighting in the dining area:

". . . when the table has the same light all over it, and has the same light level on the walls around it, the light does nothing to hold people together; the intensity of feeling is quite likely to dissolve; there is little sense that there is any special kind of gathering. But when there is a soft light, hung low over the table, with dark walls around so that this one point of light lights up people's faces and is a focal point for the whole group, then a meal can become a special thing indeed, a bond, a communion."

"An overlit room is a horror for dining."
—BILLY BALDWIN

- Don't buy a chandelier with hard-to-clean, dust-attracting glass globes or prisms. A simple, elegant fixture is easier to maintain.
- Install a dimmer switch and use candles to set the mood and hide the dust.
- Buy beeswax candles; they're smokeless and burn longer than paraffin.
- Slip bobeches (small, transparent drip dishes) around the base of candles to catch melting wax.
- Prevent candle wax from being blown over the table by extinguishing tapers with a candle snuffer.
- Trim long candlewicks so they don't burn lopsidedly or clog the center well with wax.
- Refrigerate candles before using; they'll burn longer.

DETAILS

- Use giant napkins to protect laps, seat cushions, and floors.
- Fold, don't ring. Napkin rings are pretty on napkins, but once they're off, they end up cluttering the table.
- Avoid floor-length tablecloths for dining. They look elegant, but it takes more grace than most of us are blessed with to avoid stepping on them or catching our chair legs in their hems.
- Ban table linens that need heavy starching and ironing, or at least limit them to a table runner or a short topper.
- Silver is pretty but requires frequent polishing to stay that way. Wrap it well in tarnishproof cloth and bring it out only for state occasions.

"And Keep Those Elbows off the Table!"

Table manners have long separated the cultured from the uncouth. Before cutlery appeared on European tables in the late sixteenth century, the masses grabbed food full fist, while nobles delicately scooped with only their first three fingers, keeping their pinkies and ring fingers clean.

Medieval knights set themselves apart from the platter sharers by eating from their own plates and drinking from individual goblets. But up until the early nineteenth century, common folk shared communal dishes. A medieval Miss Manners warned: "When everyone is eating from the same dish, you should take care not to put your hand into it before those of higher rank have done so."

When cutlery became fashionable, it was routine to pick one's teeth with the knife at the table. Legend has it that Cardinal Richelieu found this practice so repulsive he had the tips of his table knives filed down. But the cardinal may have had less control over other practices common to the times, like blowing one's nose in the tablecloth, expectorating, and spitting bones and bits of gristle on the floor.

- Rubber darkens silver, so never dry it on a rubber mat.
- Replace high-maintenance silver with easy-care glass, ceramic, alloys, and stainless-steel pieces.
- Buy top-quality stainless steel. The best is mixed with 18 percent chromium and 8 percent nickel. Chromium gives the steel hardness and nickel gives it luster.
- When buying stainless-steel flatware, look for a smooth and uniform finish that's easy to clean.
- Avoid buying china with gold trim. Gold smears in hot water and has to be washed *very* carefully.
- Crystal is also temperamental; a hot wash followed by a cool rinse can cause it to crack.
- Consolidate dishes and glassware with large, wide-mouthed, stemmed glasses that can be used for water, wine, juice, cold soups, and desserts.

EASIER SETUP AND CLEANUP

• Photocopy a diagram of a table setting for young or forgetful table setters.

• Teach young table setters that fork and left have four letters while knife, spoon, glass, and right have five.

• Use a tea cart or a serving tray to set and clear the table quickly and easily.

• Fill a few dishpans with soapy water before dinner: one for glassware and silver, one for plates, and one for pots and pans. Soak pots before dinner and the rest before dessert.

• Accept all offers to clean up. Most people like to be part of the action, and there's often more camaraderie in the kitchen after dinner than during it in the dining room.

• Entertain in warm weather on the patio and let the birds clean the crumbs.

THE
BATHROOM

Mildew on the walls, towels on the floor, and ring around the tub are enough to make you want to give up indoor plumbing.

But the bathroom can be easier to keep clean with a few preventative smarts, some sensible storage, and plenty of easy-to-maintain surfaces.

CONDITION

Invest in an in-house water softener. Hard water leaves spots on porcelain and chrome, clogs showerheads, and damages water-using appliances like dental irrigators, facial saunas, and vaporizers. Soft water is a solvent, so cleaning products go further and require less elbow grease.

BLOW DRY

• Sunlight and fresh air are good antidotes to the mold and mildew that muck up the works, but when there's no window and/or the weather won't cooperate, use a good exhaust fan to keep decay at bay.

• Many fans are set to go on with the flick of the light switch, but since they're usually noisy and not always necessary, they often go unused. A better alternative is to install a moisture-activated fan. One made by Braun automatically responds to sudden changes in humidity, as when the shower goes on or the tub fills. It turns itself off when it senses it has dried things up sufficiently.

CUT

The bathroom often ends up a storeroom for cosmetic counter regrets: the cologne only the dog responds to, the face cream that clogs pores, the hair accessory that was going to end all those bad hair days. None of it gets better with age, and it crowds out the good stuff. Toss what you don't use to make room for what you do.

PUT IT AWAY

• Clear the counter. A clutter-free counter is easier to keep clean than a counter that looks like a Clinique display. Store cosmetics, toiletries, and hair dryers out of sight when not in use.

• Don't overstock without first considering where it's all going to fit. A bushel of toilet paper may be a bargain, but not when it takes over the bathroom.

• Store bath toys, soap, brushes, and the like either in a vinyl-clad bath basket that hangs over the tub, or in a dishpan under the vanity.

• Provide plenty of closed storage space. Cabinets and drawers present a neater solution to storage than open shelves.

• Plan for both shallow and deep drawers. Shallow drawers are best for cosmetics, combs, and brushes. Deep drawers are good for hair dryers and other bulky items.

• Use dividers or plastic cutlery trays to separate and organize cosmetics and toiletries.

• Mount a vinyl-coated wire rack on the inside of a cabinet door to organize and store stuff.

• Install a hook on the back of the door for a damp robe and shower cap.

• Hang a shelf above the door to store extra towels.

• If there's no storage shelf in the shower, slip a caddy over the nozzle head to keep shampoo, conditioner, razor, and such off the floor.

• Label shelves, bins, and baskets so things get put back where they belong.

• Store together items that are used together: hair dryer, mousse, and styling brush, for example; and razor, shaving cream, and aftershave.

• Keep items used daily within close reach, the rest on higher or lower shelves.

THE TOILET

• Forgo fuzzy seat and tank covers. They collect grime and germs, add to the wash load, and do nothing for the decor.

• Bare is beautiful, but if cold feet demand a rug in front of the toilet, make sure it's mid-toned or patterned and machine washable.

• Keep a toilet brush in a caddy adjacent to the toilet so it's available to all. A frequent swish puts off a weekly scrub.

• Use an in-tank cleaner that slowly releases chlorine bleach into the bowl. Just make sure the bowl is flushed at least daily so the cleaner won't damage tank parts.

• Or try a weekly overnight soak of cheap white vinegar to keep the bowl stain-free.

• The area around the bowl can be a challenge to keep clean if there are little boys in the household. Cleaning consultant and author Don Aslett suggests painting a red dot near the bottom of the back of the bowl as an "irresistible challenge" to aim for. It works for big boys too.

THE TUB

What a tub is made out of determines how easy it is to maintain. Fiberglass scratches, yellows, and turns porous over time, so it's difficult to keep looking decent, although some who have it find a coat of car wax helps it stay cleaner longer.

Acrylic and enameled steel are a little more durable and easy to maintain, but enamel-coated cast iron is the crème de la crème of tubs. It doesn't chip, is slow to scratch, and has a deep, rich finish that cleans up nicely.

- Whatever the material, encourage users to swish their hands or feet around the water line to loosen bathtub ring before they pull the plug. A few licks of the sponge should easily finish the job, before gunk hardens into plaque.
- Install a hand-held shower to rinse the tub as well as soapy heads and bodies.
- Use water-softener beads instead of bath oil to prevent bathtub ring.
- When shopping for a tub, avoid a sunken model; they're killers to climb in and out of, bathe children in, and clean.

Physics lesson: "When a body is submerged in water, the phone rings."

THE SHOWER

- Cover the ceiling above the shower with tile or the shower enclosure material to avoid a blistered, rotting ceiling.
- Replace clear glass with a frosted door, since the latter doesn't show water and soap spots.
- If there's a shower curtain instead of a door, move the rod up to ceiling level. The higher positioning better protects the room from splatters and gives a more graceful effect.
- Use a fabric curtain with a vinyl liner. It's prettier than plain vinyl and looks fresher longer.
- Keep the door or curtain open for a few minutes after a shower to dispel moisture.
- Keep the curtain closed the rest of the time so mold doesn't grow in its folds.
- Store a squeegee in the shower to wipe down wet walls so there's no soap-scum buildup.

• Cover shower and tub drains with vinyl strainers to trap hair. Tissue off after each shampoo.

THE SINK, COUNTER, AND FAUCET

• If you are remodeling, buy a sink wide enough to contain dripping elbows and deep enough to minimize splashing the counter and mirror.

• Invest in a one-piece molded countertop/sink/ back-splash combination made of Corian. It's the easiest to maintain, since there are no rims or seams to collect dirt, and even hair dye wipes off Corian.

• Replace deteriorating faucets with epoxy-coated models. Epoxy faucets resemble porcelain but don't crack. They also don't corrode or show smudges like chrome and other metals. Plus, they come clean easily with just a little soap and water.

• If you're long on cosmetics and short on space, store them on a plastic countertop tray so they're easy to move at cleaning time.

• Hang a shelf under an eye-level mirror in a child's room, and keep it stocked with brushes and combs so less hair ends up in the bathroom sink.

THE FLOOR

• Cover the floor with sheet vinyl in a subtle or splashy pattern. Steer clear of solid white, black, or a checkerboard pattern of both.

• Hair is the most noticeable dropping on a bathroom floor. If there are mostly blondes in the family, go with a lighter color floor. Brunettes need a darker color, and a combination household benefits from a pattern combining both light and dark tones.

• Minimize hairy floors by encouraging long-haired family members to dry their locks naturally in the sun. I had a neighbor who used to send her teenage daughter outside to dry her waist-long hair in front of the air conditioner.

• Avoid vinyl tiles, since water can seep under each seam.

• Consider installing a floor drain to slurp up spills. Noted bath and kitchen designer Nancy Blandford admits it had never occurred to her to install floor drains until she had children. "Our kids flood out the bathroom every time they take a bath," she said. "I'm beginning to think a floor drain is a good idea in most bathrooms."

• Prevent a water-splattered floor by hanging a weighted shower curtain.

• If the floor is carpeted, lay a washable rug in front of the sink to protect the carpet from cosmetic and toiletry spills.

• Get magazines off the floor and into a wall-mounted rack.

THE WALLS

• Don't wallpaper a steamy, heavily used bathroom, since paste has a nasty habit of coming apart at the seams in high humidity.

• If you like patterned walls, consider stenciling. It's easier than it looks, and templates and brushes are available at most craft, paint, and home centers.

• Use either an oil-based alkyd or water-based acrylic paint for walls.

• Have the paint mixed with a mildewcide if the room has a moisture problem.

• Use a high-gloss finish if walls are in good shape and a semigloss finish if they're not. The higher gloss repels soil best, but it also shows up dents and dings.

THE WINDOW

• Use frosted, sandblasted, stained, or etched glass to admit light, provide privacy, and cut down on cleaning.

• Check out liquid crystal technology where tiny crystals are encased between two sheets of tempered glass. Flip a switch and the glass is clear; flip it back and the crystals provide frosted privacy.

• Consider glass-block windows. They not only provide privacy and light, but deaden street noise and insulate as effectively as thermal pane glass without the cleaning hassle of drapes or blinds.

• Keep window coverings permanently pristine by ordering windows with blinds sandwiched between double panes of glass. Otherwise avoid blinds. They're murder to clean.

• If you have conventional windows, hang vinyl shades that draw from the bottom up to ensure privacy.

Towels

• Assign each family member his or her own towel color to identify "droppers" and cut down on laundry. Buy coordinating colors for the prettiest effect—all jewel tones, primaries, or pastels.

• Buy dark or printed towels for children, since they're most likely to stain them.

THE GUEST TOWEL DILEMMA

No one ever uses those dainty little guest towels we all set out for company. Etiquette mavens blame it on mothers' admonishments to "save" them. Whether that's the case or it's the worry about who or what has already touched them, most guests, it seems, would rather wipe their hands on their clothes than violate the linen.

A better alternative is a roll of plain white paper towels mounted on an unobtrusive holder near the sink. Paper towels are cheap, sanitary, and so user-friendly they may encourage users to give the sink and counter a once-over before they leave. Plus, they're exactly where you need them when a more thorough cleaning is called for.

• Hang towel hooks, rings, or bars high on walls and doors for adults and low on walls for children—hooks and rings take up less space than bars.

• Don't layer hand towels and facecloths over bath towels, since you'll have to move them every time you want the big one on the bottom.

• Roll stored towels and washcloths. Rolling is not only easier than folding, it takes up less space.

KEEPING UP APPEARANCES

• When remodeling or replacing fixtures, choose neutral, "soapy" colors like white, beige, and ivory to camouflage soap scum and mineral deposits on counters, sinks, tubs, and showers. Neutral colors are also cheaper, as well as timeless. Bright towels, paint, and accessories will give the room color and can be easily and cheaply changed.

• Use a pump dispenser on the counter, in the shower, and by the tub to avoid soap slime. Buy an opaque bottle to hide finger marks. Or place a small sponge in the soap dish under the soap; when it's saturated it can clean a tub and its occupant.

• Choose towel bars and toilet paper holders in a no-maintenance, antique brass finish.

• Stash a bottle of glass cleaner in a cabinet for quick mirror, sink, or counter touch-ups.

• Save elbow grease by letting cleaning products marinate on surfaces.

THE TOILET-PAPER REPORT

Northern, the toilet-paper maker, has come up with the following sociological findings on bathroom use:

• Americans, on average, skip to the loo six times a day, adding up to forty-seven minutes in a twenty-four-hour period.

• Women spend more time there than men; or ap-

ORDER OF THE BATH

Bathrooms have been in and out of fashion for centuries. Nearly four thousand years ago in Crete, the royal court began and ended its day in large, luxurious bathrooms, complete with flushing toilets, shell-shaped sinks, and elegant tubs into which water was hydraulically pumped from nearby reservoirs.

While conquering Greeks regarded such rooms as frivolous, the Romans conducted state, business, and social affairs in opulent public baths. Unfortunately their "social affairs" got out of hand, so bathing took on a moral, then a health stigma. For almost fifteen centuries, from peasant to ruler, Europe went virtually unwashed. The wealthy perfumed their bodies. The poor just stank.

Legend has it that Queen Isabella of Spain boasted she bathed twice in her life, once at birth and once before her marriage.

Louis XIV of France feared bathing brought on illness, so other than an occasional dip, he avoided it.

An "earthy aura" was even considered desirable by some. On his triumphant return from a campaign in Egypt, Napoleon sent the following to Josephine, "Home in three weeks. Don't bathe."

In 1837, when Queen Victoria came to the throne, there wasn't a single bathroom in Buckingham Palace. However, when nineteenth-century social reformers began to realize the link between disease and lack of hygiene, the bathroom came in from the cold.

The "little room at the top of the stairs" has evolved into a large and luxurious space with enough amenities to please a monarch. The trouble is, the slaves and the servants are gone, so guess who gets to clean it?

proximately thirty-two months in a lifetime versus twenty-five months for men. (Women also live longer.)

• Thirty-three percent of the women respondents say they use the room as an escape from their young charges.

• Women object most to men's leaving the seat up.

• Men object most to having to wait in line to use the facilities.

• As to what people do in there, besides the obvious, the survey reports: eating, sneaking a smoke, washing clothes, sleeping, doing homework, developing film, dancing, and making love.

THE
LIVING ROOM

The living room is a misnomer. You cook in a kitchen, sleep in a bedroom, and bathe in a bathroom, but, as Nora Ephron puts it, "What can you do in a living room?"

She writes, "My living room sits in my apartment, a silent snobbish presence, secretly contemptuous that I don't know what to do in a room that has no clear function."

It's true. The living room is the least lived-in room in the house. When there's a family room down the hall, we discourage our kids and less-than-tidy spouses from getting too comfortable here. We wouldn't dream of desecrating the place with a six-pack, a bag of Fritos, and a game of poker. The living room is kept "nice."

Some take this preservation to extremes. When I was a kid, my friend Sally's living-room upholstery was swathed in plastic that never came off, even for company. I could never figure out what her mom was saving it for. She even kept the cellophane on the lamp shades.

When we were teenagers, her father built a paneled rumpus room in the basement, complete with refrigerator, powder room, and a huge bar as its centerpiece. "Dave's Rathskeller" he called it. It wasn't for Sally and her friends—we were now confined to the bedroom—it was for her parents, who entertained there. I guess they didn't want anyone sweating all over the plastic upstairs.

The upper classes of an older era seemed to know what to do in a living room, or drawing room, as they called it. At least that was the case in the Bellamy household on PBS's *Upstairs Downstairs.*

The Bellamys' drawing room holds separate desks where the couple sees to their correspondence in the morning. Guests are received in the afternoon where tea is served amid dark walls, oak bookcases, and aged leather. Brandy is served by Hudson after dinner in front of the fire. How civilized. And how lived-in.

The butler and parlor maid may be gone, but if we made the room more functional and less fragile, we'd get more mileage out of it. Some ideas:

MAKING IT FUNCTIONAL

- Arrange the room the way you want to use it daily rather than for occasional entertaining. Studies show the average household spends about 95 percent of its time with immediate family or alone and only 5 percent with company.
- If there's a family room with a TV, make the living room a quiet retreat for reading, conversation, and catching a few Zs. Professional house cleaner Marie Ruiz finds a room without a TV stays cleaner longer. "There's something about TV watching that generates all kinds of messy habits," said Ruiz.
- Use flexible, multipurpose pieces to avoid overfurnishing. A partner's desk, for example, can accommodate two and can be used for intimate dinners, puzzle working, and games. A sofa table with drop-down leaves can be extended for a number of uses.
- Use lightweight stacking tables near seating. They're convenient landing pads for books and cups and can be moved around easily.
- Use bright lights for reading and working, soft lights for conversation and relaxing, and flattering light for parties. Put them all on dimmers to control the mood and hide the dust.
- Provide a reading light for every seat.

ELABORATE TREATMENTS, ELABORATE CARE

Living-room windows tend to be overdone with great swaths of fabric that need to be vacuumed or taken down, dry-cleaned, and hung again.

Since window coverings collect dust and dirt that seep in from the outside, you can save yourself a lot of trouble by hanging either washable curtains, shoji screens, or wide-blade shutters. If privacy and fading aren't a problem, a simple swag of gracefully draped, washable fabric will soften the glass, frame the view, and welcome the light.

REDECORATING

• Buy a sofa with loose back and seat cushions. Loose cushions are not only more comfortable but can be flipped when they are soiled or worn. I was seduced by a sexy sofa with a tight, curved back a few years ago. Had I chosen a model with back cushions instead, I could have easily turned them over and hidden the water stains that resulted from a leaky roof.

• Look for zippered pillow or cushion covers so pillows and cushions are easy to spot-clean.

• Avoid solid-color upholstery fabrics. Prints, plaids, and flecks make spots and wear less noticeable.

• Choose upholstered pieces with skirts. Unlike pieces with bare legs, skirted furniture is less apt to attract dust and lint underneath, and if it does, who knows and who cares?

• Avoid down filling. It's soft and cushy, but it loses its shape and, according to exterminators, is a favorite hideout for moths and carpet beetles. Dense foam, wrapped in polyester batting, is a better bet.

• Choose sofas and upholstered chairs in simple, gimmick-free shapes that can be easily slipcovered.

• Stay clear of tassels, fringes, and buttons. Clean design is classic and easier to care for.

• Buy simple, unpleated, unruffled lamp shades. Dust collects in pleats and flounces.

• Use a free-standing bookcase, screens, or other dividers to create cozy nooks and to hide a potentially messy area like a desk.

STORAGE

• Plan for plenty of closed storage; the more there is, the easier it is to keep order.

• House a stereo and its equipment, as well as bar ware, reading material, and other stuff in a large, handsome armoire.

• Cover a side table with a floor-length cloth for a handy place to stash the newspaper and other clutter when company comes.

"The natural sport of England is obstacle racing. People fill their rooms with useless and cumbersome furniture and spend the rest of their lives trying to dodge it."

—SIR HERBERT BEERBOHM TREE

DAMAGE CONTROL

• Save yourself grief by putting away the breakables until the children are grown.

• Use arm caps to protect the most vulnerable spots from soil and wear. If they're made out of the upholstery fabric and fit snugly, they're hardly noticeable.

• Protect fabrics with a spray-on finish like Scotchgard.

• Serve guests only clear soft drinks and white wine. Red wine, especially inexpensive varieties, stains fabrics. According to the 3M company, cheaper wines contain higher concentrations of colorant.

• Toss a washable quilt, afghan, or blanket over the sofa when there's anyone under twenty-one in the entourage.

• Keep upholstered and wood furnishings clear of drying radiator and vent heat.

• Avoid using an ottoman as a coffee table. It's a popular decorating look, but with the possibility of spills and stains, a bad idea. Besides, food and feet don't mix.

• Place a densely patterned, easily cleaned rug under

"It takes a heap o'
livin' in a house t'
make it home."
—EDGAR GUEST

the coffee table, since this is where most spots occur on wall-to-wall carpeting.

• Place glass tops or use a urethane finish on wood tables. Or keep a good supply of coasters on hand. The century-old Moana Surfrider hotel in Hawaii protects its mahogany veranda tables from spills and burns with glass tops that allow the beauty of the wood to show through.

• Consider using a color like russet red, forest green, or chocolate on the walls. Deep shades are cozy, show off art and collections nicely, and hide finger marks.

EASIER CLEANING

• Showcase collections behind glass to cut down on dusting. Interior designer Diane Just often groups her clients' collections in shadow boxes or Plexiglas cubes to enhance them. A glass-fronted cabinet works well too.

• Place tabletop paraphernalia on trays that can be easily lifted for dusting.

• Use wall instead of table and floor lamps, so there are fewer items to move and clean around. Buy the kind with metal sleeves to hide the electrical cords.

• Don't overfurnish. Empty space makes maintenance easier and gives a sense of roominess.

• Include a wastebasket. Every room needs one.

BUYING WOOD FLOORING

Appealingly warm and remarkably durable, wood is the most popular floor in today's living room. If you're about to lay some boards:

• Buy heavily grained, distressed wood. Wood comes in various grades from "clear" to "common." "Clear" is the most expensive, since it has the fewest natural markings. "Common" is the cheapest, since it is full of knots, curls, and graining. But since nature's markings camouflage man-made nicks, scratches, and scuff marks, cheaper, in this case, is better.

THE END OF WASHING WINDOWS?

Windows get dirty easily, especially in bad weather, but Weather Shield Manufacturing claims their new window glass, Kleen-Shield, stays cleaner longer than ordinary glass. Treated with a polymer similar to Teflon, it creates a nonstick surface that promises to resist bird droppings, rain splatters, and anything else that can soil a window.

Windows can also be kept cleaner longer with deep overhangs, awnings, or European-type roll shutters.

If the view is ugly and there's a privacy problem, stained or frosted glass can solve the problem beautifully with a minimum of maintenance.

• Avoid beveled edges common to parquet patterns. A plank or strip floor is easier to maintain, since it has no grime-catching grooves.

• Look for a factory finish where each coat of polyurethane has been exposed to a hardening dose of ultraviolet light.

MAINTAINING WOOD FLOORS

• Stain a wood floor a medium shade so lint, dust, and dirt will be less apparent.

• Coat the floor with a low-gloss, long-lasting urethane finish (if it doesn't already have one) so it won't need waxing or polish.

• Strip wax before applying urethane, since wax makes the finish peel.

• Don't bleach. Bleaching softens wood and makes it more vulnerable to scratches and dents. And a pale floor shows dirt and scuff marks to boot.

• Explore the possibilities of a faux or pickled finish on heavily damaged wood. The added pattern hides dents, as well as dust and dirt, beautifully.

• Avoid rubber-backed rugs and pads. Rubber stains and is nonventilated. Wood needs to breathe.

- Use plastic casters, glides, or felt caps on furniture legs to avoid scratches.
- Protect floors when moving furniture by slipping socks over the legs or positioning a thick beach towel underneath.
- Use a touch of shoe polish in a matching shade to hide nicks and scratches.
- Slip off high heels before walking on wood. A high-heeled 130-pounder packs 2,000 pounds of dent potential.
- Slip off all shoes at the door. There's enough dirt generated inside without importing it.
- Have the family wear cotton or wool socks. Terry Kawasaki finds her three kids polish the floor just going about their daily business.
- Avoid one-step clean-and-shine products. The theory is that dirt and grit are loosened and retained in the mop. In reality, they are trapped in the finish. A mop dampened with diluted white vinegar will clean and leave a subtle shine.

OTHER FLOORS

- Buy wall-to-wall carpeting in a tight, low-pile weave with twisted heat-set fibers.
- Choose a light to medium shade of carpet with dark flecks to disguise spots.
- Use a solid or slightly variegated ceramic tile in a neutral go-with-anything, hide-everything color.
- Install a tile baseboard to protect the wall; it won't get nicked and gouged like conventional wood.
- Remember, a floor is something you walk on, not eat on. Scratches and dust are inevitable, so relax.

SECRETS OF A CLEAN FIRE

Too many fireplaces are unused because people dislike having to clean up a mess; yet curling up in front of a crackling fire is one of life's small pleasures. To enjoy the warmth and avoid the fuss:

"My other house is cleaner."

—WHAT TO EMBROIDER ON A THROW PILLOW

• Burn well-seasoned, leaf-producing hardwoods like oak, maple, and birch. Hardwoods burn longer with less smoke, ash, and creosote than needle-bearing softwoods like pine, spruce, and fir.

• Bring in only what you need when you need it. A basket full of logs by the hearth may add a homey touch, but it may also add undesirable hoarders like roaches and termites.

• Use a heavy-duty firewood tote. It not only makes bringing the wood in easier but prevents scattering of crumbling bark and dirt.

• Consider buying artificial logs—paper-encased compactions of sawdust and wax. They produce less creosote and smoke than the real thing.

• Open the damper and check out the chimney periodically for obstructions. A bird nest could result in a room full of smoke and scrambled eggs on the grate.

• Keep the fire screen closed once the flames start licking the logs.

• Place a mat or a carpet remnant over adjacent flooring, since sparks can escape when logs are stoked or added.

• Don't be too quick to dispose of ashes. A good fire needs at least a two-inch carpet of ash under the grate so it starts faster and radiates heat into the room.

• When you do get around to taking out the ashes, make sure they're cold. Then open the damper, so the dust will be drawn up and out the chimney instead of into the room.

Chapter 19

THE
FAMILY ROOM

"The rooms that are lived in are the ones we find most comforting."

—ALEXANDRA
STODDARD

The family room ought to be comfortable for couch potatoes as well as tough enough for roughnecks. So it's got to have furnishings, floors, and fabrics that can roll with the punches without looking like they belong in a gym.

HARD GOODS: TABLES, CHAIRS, AND DESKS

• Outfit the room with distressed country-style furniture that can be further abused to mellowed perfection.

• Buy sturdy pieces with abuse-tolerant plastic laminate tops. Plastic laminate is cheaper than wood, and you won't flinch when someone props her feet up on the coffee table and paints her toenails.

• Look for a trunk that can store stuff and be used as an ottoman, bench, or coffee table. I know one family that stores all its board games in an oversized footlocker. When family members are not using it as a footrest, bench, or cup holder, they sit on the floor and play everything from poker to Pictionary on it.

• Cover ready-made or easily assembled plywood boxes with carpeting, wood floor tiles, or sheets of pregrouted ceramic tile for almost indestructible coffee and end tables.

• Back a sofa with a narrow table and a couple of chairs so you can work on a project while watching TV.

SOFT GOODS: SOFAS AND UPHOLSTERED CHAIRS

• Lure little gymnasts off the sofa with plenty of good-sized floor pillows or mats, slipcovered in washable cases. And put a trampoline or a jungle gym in the back-yard.

• Install casters on the sofa and other heavy pieces so they can be pushed to one side for workouts, dancing, or play.

• Give a recliner enough clearance so it doesn't scuff and dent the wall.

• Family-room fabrics take a licking, so buy, uphol-ster, or slipcover the sofa and chairs in bulletproof goods like denim, canvas, crushed velvet, or corduroy. Have them quilted for extra durability.

• Steer clear of solid dark and solid light colors. Like a suit that displays dandruff, navy and black upholstery show every speck of dust and dog hair; white and pastels show everything else.

• Use medium colors in allover prints. Tweeds, flo-rals, and plaids work well, as do batik, African mud cloth, and other primitive prints with their deep colors and strong patterns.

• If you prefer solid-color fabrics, use nubby tex-tures that create a soil-hiding light-and-shadow effect. I have a sofa covered in solid taupe textured velvet that has outlasted a couple of Mary Lou Rettons and a Dagwood Bumstead and still looks good.

CUT FROM THE RIGHT CLOTH

For longer wear with less care, consider where the fabric will be used. Chairs and sofas are subject to the friction of sitting, reclining, and shifting, so good abrasion qualities are important. Window coverings are vulnerable to dam-age from ultraviolet rays, so a fiber with good sun resis-tance will hold up longer.

Fibers are divided into three categories: naturals, synthetics, and blends. Naturals are generally comfortable, age gracefully, and clean easily, but have a tendency to shrink, fade, and attract soil. Synthetics are mostly soil and abrasion resistant, but often difficult to clean and can be cold and scratchy. Blends are designed to bring out the best of both. A small percentage of nylon can improve the performance of wool, for instance, and a bit of polyester can take the shrinkage out of cotton.

Among the naturals:

Cotton   Comfortable, strong, and versatile. It has excellent pilling resistance and a pretty good resistance to abrasion and sunlight. Blending it with a synthetic makes it stand up to soil.

Wool   Warm, resilient, and resistant to abrasion and fading. Other than its susceptibility to moths and mildew, it's easy to maintain, especially when blended with a synthetic.

Linen   Crisp and cool, it's nonstatic and resists moths and soil. But it stretches and wrinkles easily unless blended with more stable fabrics.

Silk   Supple and surprisingly strong. It drapes gracefully, dyes beautifully, and adds an iridescent luster to other fabrics. However, it has poor abrasion resistance, spots easily, and is difficult to clean.

Leather   Though technically not a fiber, leather is strong, with excellent abrasion resistance. But dust, grit, and grime crack it, and it needs special conditioning to stay supple.

The more widely used synthetics:

Nylon   The Hulk Hogan of fibers, it's soil, mildew, and abrasion resistant. Highly versatile, it can produce everything from woolly tweeds to silky velvets. It has a tendency to pill and fade, however, but it adds strength to anything it touches.

Polyester   Crisp, strong, and wrinkle-free, it holds

KNOW YOUR CODE

All upholstered furniture manufactured since 1970 comes with a cleaning code. Check the tag on the underside of a cushion or under the piece itself and you'll see a "WS," "W," "S," or an "X."

WS: the most desirable, since the piece can be cleaned either with a water-based cleaner like an upholstery foam or a dry-cleaning solvent

W: use a water-based cleaner

S: use a solvent only

X: nothing will work but brushing or vacuuming

The code isn't always what it seems, however, since some manufacturers slap on an "X" rating to cover themselves should the cleaning process go awry.

---

up well to sunlight, abrasion, and water-based stains. It can feel a little stiff, and it absorbs grease stains, but with the addition of cotton, it's a marriage made in heaven.

Rayon   Silky and inexpensive, it has the look and feel of a natural and some of the attributes of a synthetic. It drapes well and resists moths but is subject to abrasion, fading, and wrinkling. It's at its best when combined with nylon, cotton, or wool.

Acrylic   Soft, as well as wrinkle and abrasion resistant, it retains its shape well but tends to darken with exposure to sunlight. It repels soil, cleans easily, and blends beautifully with most fibers.

Acetate   Inexpensive, sunfast, and drapes gracefully, but will wrinkle and has low abrasion resistance unless blended with stronger fibers.

Olefin   Abrasion, sun, and soil resistant, but it pills and is sometimes scratchy to the touch.

Vinyl   Not a fiber, vinyl upholstery is a fabric-backed plastic that resists most stains. Body oils and perspiration harden it, and it feels cold, so it's not the best sofa covering. But it's excellent for chair seats, benches, and ottomans, as long as there are no paws with claws around.

FABRIC FACTS

• The closer the weave, the more durable the fabric.
• A fabric with a pattern woven into it is stronger than one with a pattern printed on its surface.
• A high price often reflects high fashion rather than high performance.

PUTTING FABRIC TO THE TEST

• Rub it with an eraser to see if it pills.
• If it's bonded, rub the backing together to see if it flakes.
• Stretch the fabric lengthwise, crosswise, and diagonally. A durable fabric will bounce back, while an unstable fabric will stay bent out of shape.

SPRAY-ON PROTECTION

Spray-on fabric guards protect our investment and make housekeeping easier. And while they don't make fabrics stainproof, they do make spills and dirt sit on the finish, at least initially, rather than soak into the fibers.

There are two types: silicone, which resists water-based stains such as grape juice and wine; and fluorochemical, which resists both water- and oil-based stains (such as salad dressing and butter).

Most upholstery fabric houses spray their goods before they leave the factory, so when you buy a sofa, that pitch for "extra protection" is an overkill, according to industry insiders.

It's a good idea to spray the piece after it has been cleaned a few times, however. The 3M company recommends saturating fabrics with Scotchgard at least after every third cleaning. The results are cumulative; less is needed with successive applications.

If you're not sure the fabric has ever been treated, or it has an "X" rating on the care tag, test the spray on a hidden spot to make sure it doesn't change the color.

STORAGE

A minimum of belongings and a maximum of storage is the key to family room order.

• Provide plenty of closed storage for games, toys, tapes, magazines, and exercise gear, and open storage for books and sound equipment.

• House the TV and accompanying gear in an entertainment center. Keep equipment neatly organized in baskets and bins, since the cabinet will be open much of the time.

• Keep a handsome box on the coffee or sofa table to hold the remote control and TV listings.

• Position a couple of free-standing storage closets on either side of a wall-centered window to create the needed depth for a window seat. Add a flip-up lid to the seat for even more stashing space.

• Include plenty of child-height shelves so the kids can easily put away their toys, games, and books.

• Place a basket under a reading table to hold the overflow of magazines and other reading matter.

THE FLOOR

The family room floor sees a lot of action—so it's crucial that it be tough, soil-hiding, and easy to clean.

• Choose sheet vinyl, wood, or tile in a color and pattern that will hide wear and tear.

• Choose an unglazed tile that can be sealed in place rather than one with a factory finish. Tile with a factory finish is difficult to repair.

• Consider using a low-napped, tightly woven, commercial grade of carpeting. Commercial grades have lots of subtle soil-hiding patterns that camouflage the heaviest use.

• Keep the floor cleaner longer by stashing outdoor shoes at the entrance, where they belong.

WINDOWS AND WALLS

• Line the room in shelves and cabinets to increase storage and absorb noise.

• Consider heavily grained paneling or a printed vinyl wall covering. Brick and barn siding are also easy to maintain, provided they're not too close to a grease-generating kitchen.

• Go with the flow. I know a woman whose apartment walls were in such bad shape, she played up the crumbling-villa effect by sponging on a couple of shades of thinned ocher and terra-cotta paint in cloud formations, then penciled marblelike veins along the cracks.

• Paint windowsills and frames with high-gloss enamel so dust and dirt don't stick.

• Renew worn weather-stripping around windows to keep out airborne dust.

• Hang wide-blade hardwood shutters in a medium dust-hiding color or stain for a clean, uncluttered look. Shutters also hide smudged and splattered windows while they admit air and light.

LIGHTING

• Replace table and floor lamps with overhead, undercabinet, and wall lighting, so cords aren't tripped over, lamps aren't overturned, and cleaning is easier.

• Install ceiling track lights to illuminate art, plants, and projects. Lighting designers recommend installing a couple of tracks two to three feet from the wall rather than one track down the center of the room.

DAMAGE CONTROL

• Fix scratched and torn vinyl with an automobile upholstery repair kit.

• Catch spills before they become stains with a thick *white* towel. A colored towel could introduce a dye stain.

• Protect a good sofa or hide a hideous one with a heavy flannel or percale king-sized sheet. Toss it over the sofa, and smooth and tuck it into cushion crevices. For a semipermanent solution, secure it with upholsterer's tacks or sew a few strategically placed buttons on the sofa and buttonholes on the sheet.

• Fold a small baby quilt or stadium blanket over the back of a wing chair to protect it from overconditioned, moussed, and sprayed heads.

• Confine food to the kitchen and dining areas, or at least to a family-room table. Television seems to generate mindless snacking and dribbling all over the furniture and floor.

• Consider moving the TV to the breakfast room or kitchen if the household can't watch without noshing all over the upholstery.

• Take it easy. While it's always good to encourage neatness, this is one place we should be able to put up our feet and let down our hair. Comfort, relaxation, and fun should take precedence over law and order.

"The art of being wise is the art of knowing what to overlook."
—WILLIAM JAMES

Chapter 20

THE MASTER
BEDROOM

"After making the bed two days in a row the thrill is gone."
—ART BUCHWALD

It's the first place we see in the morning, and the last we see at night. When it's a mess, it can muddle our days and darken our dreams. When it's tidy, it can shut out the world, soothe the psyche, and nurture the soul. So it pays to set it up so it's easy to keep clean, serene, and organized.

CLUTTER CONTROL

Because we do everything from sleep to work out here, the place often becomes a stockroom of clutter. We need to be vigilant about what comes into the room and weed out whatever isn't used on a regular basis.

FURNISHINGS

• Keep furnishings to a minimum for easy maintenance and to maneuver around the room safely in the dark. Think multipurpose: a desk that functions as a night table, a lamp that swings to light a book in bed or bills on a desk, a storage unit that houses the TV as well as tapes, books, and other equipment.

• Cover what you can with room-softening, sound-absorbing, dust-hiding fabric. I covered a parson's table on one side of the bed and an unfinished three-legged table on the other with lined, washable fabric, and topped them with glass. There's no body to polish, and no legs to attract cobwebs. Only the glass needs an occasional squirt and wipe.

• Move the bureau to the closet if there's room, or get rid of it altogether by having drawers or sliding bins and shelves built into the closet.

STORAGE

• If either you or your roommate is an avid reader, provide plenty of built-in or free-standing bookshelves. Well-stocked shelves have the added advantage of insulating and soundproofing a room.

• Don't let reading material swamp the bedside table. Only one thing can be read at a time, so keep the overflow accessible but out of sight.

• Provide plenty of closed storage for magazines, paperwork, and anything else that tends to spread itself around the room.

• Unless the bed has built-in storage drawers, think twice before stashing stuff underneath. It collects dust, is hard to get to, and has been known to stub more than a few bare toes.

• Keep a tray on the tabletop to hold the clock, reading material, glasses, and the like, so they can be moved in a swoop when the table needs a swipe.

THE BED

An unmade bed can make even the tidiest room look rumpled. The key to making it quickly and easily is to dress it simply.

• Use a big, billowy comforter over a dust ruffle to eliminate a wrinkle-prone bedspread and layers of blankets. The plumper the comforter, the less fuss with the linens underneath.

• Choose a printed comforter with a solid dust ruffle rather than the other way around. The comforter is more

THE PERFECT COMFORTER

Consumer's Union, a research group that does independent testing for Consumer Reports *magazine offers some of the following tips to its readers for choosing the perfect comforter:*

• *Judge the warmth of a comforter by comparing "loft" or plumpness. Thick comforters trap more air than thin ones, so they insulate better.*

• *Scrunch the center sections of various comforters to feel the difference between a luxurious filling and a skimpy one. Avoid testing the edges, since they're frequently more stuffed than the rest of the comforter.*

• *Comforters come in box, channel, or tufted quilting. Choose a tufted pattern for the greatest puffiness, warmth, and longevity.*

• *Choose a light color over a dark one, since the latter fades with washings.*

• *Dry-clean a down comforter. Even those labeled "washable" have been known to shrink up to six inches in width and length.*

subject to soil and wear than the dust ruffle, and a print hides it better than a solid color.

• Protect a new comforter or hide an old one by slipping it into a ready-made duvet or an envelope of two sewn sheets. This "comforter pillowcase" is easier to clean than a bulky comforter and eliminates the need for a top sheet. Buy or sew it in a reversible print for versatility.

• Keep a soft quilt, afghan, or throw at the foot of the bed to keep the bed made and protect the comforter during an afternoon nap or TV watching.

• Position the bed so there's enough space around it for easy bed making.

• Limit decorative throw pillows. They're the darlings of decorators, but they're a hassle to move every time you want to crawl into the bed or make it.

• Replace sleep pillows every few years. They collect dirt, oils, and perspiration, and often get lumpy when cleaned.

• Buy sheets with a high thread count of at least two hundred per square inch for durability and a no-iron finish for easy care.

• Mark sheets with a laundry pen at their mattress tuck-in points.

• Stuff a sheet set into one of its pillowcases to keep it together neatly. Or avoid the folding and storage hassle altogether by limiting linens to only one set that goes directly from dryer to bed.

THE HEADBOARD

The traditional wood or metal headboard does little but collect dust, dent backs, and bump heads. Padded fabric, a quilt, or a decorative rug, on the other hand, is virtually maintenance free, and if it's thick enough makes a comfortable backrest for reading. Some ideas:

• Staple polyester batting and a cut-to-fit, matching or coordinating sheet over the back of a two- to three-foot-high, one-inch-thick piece of plywood. Bolt it either to the bed frame or to the wall.

• Cover a rectangle of foam with sheeting or other fabric and hang it from a drapery rod. Have the fabric quilted for substance and add a zipper, snaps, or Velcro for easy cleaning.

• Attach a bed-to-ceiling piece of foam to the wall,

THE LAZY MAN'S GUIDE TO BED MAKING

In our house, the last one out of bed gets to make it. That's usually my husband, who in his never-ending search for efficiency has learned the art of horizontal bed making. His advice:

1. *Lie on your back, lift your bottom, and pull and smooth the fitted sheet sideways to the bottom edge of the mattress.*
2. *Pull the top sheet up under your chin, folding it over the blanket, if there is one.*
3. *Pull the comforter up as well, smoothing as you go.*
4. *Carefully slide out of bed, one leg at a time, keeping the body low.*
5. *Finish with a couple of pulls, puffs, and punches.*

mount a curtain rod just above the baseboard and another
at ceiling height behind the bed, and stretch a sheet
between them.

• Sew a slipcover cut from a matching sheet to fit an
expanding guardrail from a child's bed. No surgery is
needed, since the legs of the rail slide between the mattress and box spring. Plus, the cover comes off easily for
washing.

• Attach padding to the wall and hang a rug or a
washable quilt from a drapery pole behind the bed.

THE MATTRESS

• Keep a comfortable chair or two in the room to
preserve the mattress. Repeated sitting on the edge of the
bed damages the border wire that binds the coils.

• Turn the mattress when you change the clocks
twice a year to prevent lumps and bumps.

• Leave the tags on a new mattress so you can claim
the warranty should it cave in before you do.

• Don't use solvents to tackle mattress stains. The
chemicals in dry-cleaning fluids have been known to disin-
tegrate covers. Use soap and water instead, sparingly. Too
much moisture can ruin the stuffings.

• Don't sweat the small stuff. Protective pads, stain
repellents, frequent vacuuming, and such can keep a mattress pristine, but who really cares what it looks like? It's
covered 99 percent of the time anyway.

THE WALLS

• Go dark. Deep-toned walls are dramatic and rest-
ful and hide scrapes, scratches, and fingerprints.

• Paper walls to add style and personality to the
room and to cover dings and other damage.

• If walls are in really bad shape, apply a heavy-duty
textured paper specifically designed to cover walls that
seem beyond help.

• Order an extra roll of paper to patch future spots and tears.

• Tack up a small square of paper somewhere unobtrusive so it fades to the same shade as the rest of the wall.

• Patch a damaged spot of paper with an irregularly torn piece. A feathered edge is harder to detect than a perfectly cut rectangle or square.

> *"No matter how big, soft, or warm your bed is, you still have to get out of it."*
> —GRACE SLICK

THE CEILING

The ceiling gets more attention here than in any room. You wake on a weekend morning, or lie there flat on your back with flu, and scrutinize every crack, cobweb, and spot.

• Make an interesting camouflage with a painted mural of clouds or a constellation of stars.

• Cover with an embossed wallpaper to create a subtle foil for dust, water stains, and boredom.

LIGHTING

• Keep night tables and a desk uncluttered by hanging wall-mounted swing-arm lamps or track lights.

• Consider halogen lights. The small and powerful focused beam allows you to read in bed without (depending on his or her sensitivity) disturbing your mate.

CARPETING

Wall-to-wall carpeting is the flooring of choice here, since it feels best on bare feet, gives the room a hushed effect, and unifies it with a solid blanket of color. It's also easy to care for, since there's no broom, mop, or bucket to deal with, and it makes those dust bunnies that normally swirl around hard floors seem to disappear.

• Choose a light to mid-toned color. The lint and dust generated by bed making and dressing shows on darker tones.

• Choose a flecked design to disguise spots.

• When shopping for carpeting, take samples home. Tones change in different lighting conditions and next to other colors.

• Select carpeting with built-in stain protection. Stainmaster, Wear-Dated, and StainBlocker are some of the trade names that have sprayed or baked-in stain protection. A good-quality wool with its natural lanolin stain repellent is also an excellent choice.

• Avoid polyester and acrylic. Polyester carpeting crushes easily, while acrylic has a tendency to fuzz.

• Look for a thick, tight weave, which resists crushing and matting and forces soil to sit on the surface rather than penetrating the yarns. Bend the backs of carpet samples to see how closely yarns are tufted. Density is the key to durability.

• Lay a dense (2½ pounds per cubic foot) urethane pad ⅜ to ½ inch thick under the carpet to increase its life, absorb noise, and add bounce.

• Make sure padding is colorfast so it won't bleed into the carpet if it gets wet.

• Save the care guide that comes with new carpeting. It's a good source of stain-removal tips.

• Choose a durable carpet weave. The following range from the toughest wear to the toughest care:

1. *Level loop*   A smooth pile that includes Berber styles, the yarn forms a short, uncut loop with both ends anchored to the backing. Its pebbly surface hides footprints and furniture dents, and since it's uncut, it's less absorbent to stains. It also wears like iron.

2. *Frieze*   A tightly twisted, heat-set, low-pile yarn with a nubby effect that masks furniture indentations and the beaten path from bed to bath. This is the curly, no-fuss perm of carpets.

3. *Random sheared*   A uniform combination of cut and uncut yarns. It gives a plush look and feel without showing footprints and vacuum-cleaner tracks.

4. *Saxony*   A mix of high- and low-cut tufts that are

heat-set to retain the yarn's twist. However, the higher yarns eventually mat down to the lower yarns.

5. *Cable* An updated shag with thicker and slightly shorter yarns. It's an improvement over the hairy-looking shags of the sixties and seventies, but it still holds dirt tenaciously and needs to be frequently vacuumed and/or combed to look fluffed and presentable. The body wave of carpets.

6. *Plush or velvet* The most fragile of the lot. It crushes easily, sometimes fuzzes, and shows footprints and anything else that touches its delicate locks.

KEEPING EXISTING CARPETING CLEAN

• Grit chews up and destroys carpeting in no time, so even if you don't remove outside shoes in the rest of the house, keep them out of this inner sanctum.

• Lay a throw rug at the entrance to the room. This is the spot that shows the heaviest wear.

• Eat elsewhere. Breakfast in bed may seem like a romantic idea until you have to clean up the coffee, syrup, and blueberry stains.

• Apply a soil repellent like Scotchgard after carpets have been wet-cleaned. Be aware of its limitations, however. A soil repellent allows only about twenty-four hours' reaction time before the stain penetrates the yarns.

• Avoid carpet deodorizers. They're easy to sprinkle on but difficult to vacuum out. The powder builds up in the backing until it becomes a kind of dandruff that wet-cleaning makes worse, since moisture causes it to stick to the yarns.

HEAVY-DUTY CARPET CLEANING

With the above precautions, you can put off disruptive and often expensive deep cleaning indefinitely. When and if

---

FINDING A PROFESSIONAL CARPET CLEANER

Anybody with a machine can call himself a pro, since there is little regulation in the carpet-cleaning industry. So it pays to asks friends and neighbors for recommendations, or to get references of previous customers. Also check with the Institute of Inspection, Cleaning, and Restoration Certification; they're an independent association that trains and certifies carpet cleaners. To locate a certified company in your neighborhood, call them at 1-800-835-4624.

---

the time comes, there are three methods to choose from: steam extraction, shampooing, and dry cleaning.

1. *Steam cleaning* is recommended by major carpet manufacturers, since it doesn't require mechanical brushing that often distorts and splays yarns. Hot water is shot into the fibers; loosened dirt is then vacuumed out.

2. *Shampooing* is used by most do-it-your-selfers, since equipment is widely available for rent at grocery stores and home centers. Rotary brushes work shampoo into the yarns; the shampoo is vacuumed out when it is dry. The brushes are hard on yarns, however, and detergent residue is often left behind to dull the finish and attract more dirt.

3. *Dry cleaning* uses a powdered, granule, or liquid solvent that is sprayed, mechanically brushed into the fibers, then vacuumed—the easiest method, but not very effective on heavy-duty stains; and it is hard on the yarns.

Chapter 21

CHILDREN'S ROOMS

Clothes carpeting the floor, paraphernalia piled in the corners, and milk curdling under the unmade bed; the revolting rooms of offspring have been a problem for parents since Cain and Abel.

"You're not going anywhere till you clean this room!"
—PARENTS OF THE WORLD

We have two choices here: We can nag, holler, and threaten. Or we can try to instill a love of order when our kids are young, train them to be self-sufficient, and when they go through the rebellious stage, close the door until they fly the coop.

MOTIVATE

Involve a child in furnishing and decorating his or her room. Pride of place is a great motivator.

TRAIN

• From the time they're taking things from shelves, show them how to put things back. "Look, doesn't that look nice there?"
• As they get a little older, show them how to make their beds, dust a table, and sweep the floor.
• Work alongside them the first few years, then gradually let them take over.
• Suggest ways to keep order, but let them work out

"Correction does much, but encouragement does more."

—JOHANN WOLFGANG VON GOETHE

their own systems or live with the consequences of chaos. A lost homework paper or a soccer uniform that never made it to the washer will teach a lesson far better than a nagging parent.

- Back off. If they know you'll be in to pick up, dust, and vacuum regularly, why should they bother?
- Encourage a five- to ten-minute daily swipe. A lick a day saves Saturdays for play.

SET THE RULES

Don't nitpick, but do be specific about the unacceptable. The following are basic no-nos:

- "NO FOOD OR DRINK IN YOUR ROOM." Rotting food stinks and attracts undesirable roommates.
- "NO OUTSIDE SHOES, ESPECIALLY ATHLETIC SHOES, ALLOWED." There's enough debris on the floor without adding street scum.
- "NO CHEWING GUM ON THE BEDPOST OVERNIGHT." In fact, chewing gum shouldn't be allowed in the house, period. Gum is thought to be such an insidious mucker-upper, it's not sold in many amusement parks and in most theaters, and it is banned altogether from tidy Singapore.

ENCOURAGE REGULAR WEEDING

Children outgrow possessions as they mature, so castoffs need to be weeded regularly. Encourage organization as well as charity by having children gather outgrown clothes, toys, and books. Bring them *and* the child to a shelter or mission where they can see the need they're helping fill.

PROVIDE EASY-TO-USE STORAGE

- Keep storage simple, accessible, and safe.
- Avoid toy boxes and trunks. Nine times out of ten the wanted item is on the bottom of the pile and the rest

gets jumbled or dumped while the child is looking for it. The lids are also dangerous for little noggins. Use open shelves, shallow bins, and stacking baskets instead.

• Mount shelves at child-accessible height. Nothing is put back on out-of-reach shelves.

• Paint shelves different colors to encourage sorting: a blue shelf for books, a purple shelf for puzzles, a green shelf for games.

• Place bins, boxes, or dishpans on shelves to organize small items.

• Label drawers, shelves, and storage containers so that contents find their way back home. Paste on appropriate pictures for younger children.

• Buy carts with see-through wire baskets that can be rolled into the closet for easy cleanup.

• Hang a small net hammock in a corner to store and display stuffed animals and dolls.

• Borrow space from inside walls. We cut a couple of display alcoves 23 by 12 inches between the wall studs above the bed in one of the kids' rooms. They hold a clock radio, books, and treasures without cutting into floor space.

• Keep tall sports equipment and closet overflow in reasonably priced metal school lockers. They take lots of abuse and can be painted to blend or contrast with the walls. Check the Yellow Pages under "Lockers," "School Furniture," or "School Supplies."

• Organize school supplies with stacking baskets on the desk and the wall above it—or hang a three-tiered vegetable basket to catch the overflow.

• Nestle shoe boxes in drawers to organize everything from socks and underwear to bug collections.

• Mount a train or car-racing set on a sheet of fiberboard. Add handles and casters, and slide it under the bed.

• Replace flimsy boxes toys come in with sturdy containers that don't need tight repacking: beach pails for crayons and markers, see-through storage boxes or self-sealing freezer bags for action figures, and commercial ice-cream drums for blocks. The latter are free for the asking from most ice-cream shops.

• Mount a see-through hanging shoe bag above the baby's changing table to hold diapers, socks, pacifiers, and such. Later it can house small treasures.

• Add a deep dust ruffle to the bottom of the crib for hidden floor storage.

• Store and rotate toys every six months or so. Children are distracted and overwhelmed by too many—and it's harder to keep them picked up.

• Keep a brightly colored broom, dustpan, and brush in the room to encourage cleaning and to help with the gathering and depositing of tiny toys and crayons. Add a spray bottle of vinegar and water and a couple of rags for deeper cleaning as the child matures.

• Store a picnic basket near the stairs or in the hallway so the contents find their way back home.

THE CLOSET

• Streamline a young child's wardrobe. Too many clothes are not only hard to organize, they offer too many confusing choices.

• Lower closet rods to suit the height of the child.

• Store special-occasion and out-of-season clothes on a high rod.

• If siblings share a closet, paint the rod two different colors to divide it in half and keep the peace.

• It's easier to hang things on hooks and pegs than on hangers. Provide plenty of fat ones on the door and walls. Fat hooks and pegs won't dent fabrics.

• Replace wire hangers that tangle and crease with plenty of the plastic kind. Novelty hangers have been known to inspire the younger set to actually use them.

• If there's room, consider moving the dresser into the closet to free floor space and centralize the whole wardrobe.

• Instead of a hamper in the bathroom, keep a laundry basket in the closet so clothes go in as soon as they come off. If that doesn't work, mount a basketball hoop on the wall, place the laundry basket underneath, and let them perfect their shot.

• Mount a battery-operated light in the closet for maximum visibility and to discourage imaginary monsters.

"You learn many things from children. How much patience you have, for instance."

—FRANKLIN P. JONES

THE BED

• For easier bed making, buy a twin bed instead of a double. An overnight guest can sleep on a futon, on an inflatable mattress, or in a sleeping bag.

• Look for a bed with a base of built-in storage drawers.

• Replace a hard-to-manage spread and layers of blankets with a thick reversible comforter and a stay-in-place dust ruffle. If the comforter is puffy enough, those inevitable ripples and waves won't show.

• Lose the top sheet by slipping the comforter in an easily washed duvet cover.

• Give up the bed-making battle altogether and let kids sleep in washable sleeping bags on top of quilted mattress covers. All they need do is roll up the bags at the foot of the bed in the morning.

• Consider other alternatives. When my elder daughter, Kelley, outgrew her crib, she decided she was more comfortable sleeping among comforters on the floor of her playhouse than she was in her "big" bed. That was fine with us, since the bed stayed made for months. By the time her legs protruded from the playhouse door and she had to move up to the bed, she was able to straighten and smooth out the comforter herself.

FURNITURE

• Use a minimum of furnishings, so there's a maximum of open floor/play space.

CLEANUP TIME IN THE NURSERY

When the room looks like an explosion in a toy factory, make cleanup a game. Most of the following exercises, gathered from nursery school and kindergarten teachers, work as well with one child as they do with a dozen. They promote a sense of organization as well as teamwork.

• Beat the Clock. *Set the kitchen timer and see if the kids can clean up before it dings.*

• Palette Police. *Tyler puts away all the red things, Jennifer puts away all the yellow things, and Adam puts away the blue things. Variations include shapes and textures.*

• Make Your Choice. *Do you want to put away the puzzles, the trucks, or the Legos?*

• Stop the Music. *See how much they can put away before the record or tape stops.*

• The Magic Number. *"I'm going to count to a magic number to see how much you can put away before I reach it."*

• Competitive Cleaning. *"I'm going to clean out this bigger and messier cabinet while you pick up your toys. Let's see who can finish first." Give them warning. "Almost finished! La-a-a-s-st thing!"*

Make it fun, and always let them win.

• Furnish with tough stuff that can take abuse. Pieces topped with plastic laminate are always good.

• Avoid novelty furnishings. I know of a little boy who fussed, begged, and pleaded until he got a race-car bed. Two years later, he and his friends thought it was "dumb." Kids outgrow the cute and trendy quickly, and furniture is expensive to replace. Stick to the classics.

• Buy legless furniture that sits flat on the floor. Not only is it sturdier, but dust balls, toys, and other debris can't collect underneath.

• Decorate with multicolored printed fabrics. They won't show spots and stains, and a jumble of belongings will look less out of place.

• Consider a beanbag chair. It's sturdy, comfortable, and safe for furniture jumpers.

• Cut down the legs of an adult-size table and toughen it with a coat of polyurethane.

• Use a brightly painted file cabinet as a bedside table; it's just the right height and can be used to store school papers, artwork, and projects.

• Replace floor and table lamps with wall and ceiling lights. Portable lamps topple and are one more thing to clean around.

• Provide a divider when a slob shares a room with a neatnik. Ceiling-mounted draperies or a well-grounded folding screen or bookcase should cut down on squabbles.

THE WALLS

• Paint rather than paper walls. Even the toughest vinyls have seams that are tempting to pick at during bouts of illness and go-to-your-room days.

• Stick with a good semigloss enamel and let an ever-changing array of posters and pictures provide color and pattern.

• Stencil or paper a border around the top of the room, beyond temptation's reach. Or cut a long lineup of hand-in-hand people or animals from adhesive paper to add a whimsical yet inexpensive border.

• Or decorate the ceiling with a skyful of painted or self-adhesive birds, butterflies, or kites.

• Hang a roll of newsprint or shelf paper or provide a large marker board or blackboard (with dustless chalk) to give artists an acceptable canvas. Big rolls of blank newsprint can be bought cheaply at the local newspaper office.

• Provide only washable art supplies.

• Wrap a plate rack around the room about three feet off the floor to prop up the self-made masterpieces of young talents.

• Avoid tack holes and tape marks by hanging a large bulletin board for photos, postcards, and papers.

• Carpet the wall as the ultimate defense against

*"Never have children
of any kind."*
—DAVE BARRY'S
SUCCESSFUL
HOUSEKEEPING RULE #2

graffiti and fingerprints. Wall carpet also muffles noise when the boom box is part of the scene.

THE WINDOWS

• Hang coverings that are easy to operate and clean, such as vinyl shades, wooden shutters, or drip-dry curtains.

• Make simple curtains from matching sheets or pillowcases. Cut to fit, hem the bottom, and thread the rod through the existing top hem.

• Look for a shade dealer who will laminate wallpaper or fabric (from a matching sheet) to the shade.

• Jazz up a plain white shade by:

1. Adding a strip of automobile detailing tape to the bottom edge
2. Adding a border of trees, animals, or whatever, cut from self-adhesive paper
3. Stenciling a border with paint
4. Letting your child create a mural with markers
5. Creating a lacy border design with a hole punch
6. Gluing the motif cut from an extra sheet or pillowcase
7. Painting the window frame a bright room-coordinating color

THE FLOOR

The floor may be carpeted with clothes and toys most of the time, but underneath the mess, the material determines the maintenance.

• Lay a hard-surface floor like vinyl or polyurethaned wood to hold up to spills and provide a firm surface for block building, coloring, and car racing. A hard-surfaced floor can also be easily swept by a child.

• Provide a washable rug over a nonslip pad for comfort and warmth on a hard floor. Or pick up a few two-by-three carpet samples for little bottoms—discontinued samples can be obtained free or close to it wherever carpeting is sold.

• If wall-to-wall carpeting is preferred, look for a tightly woven, solution-dyed commercial type in a variegated medium tone. It's easy care and provides a warm, soft surface for kids who spend much of their time on the floor. Carpeting needs to be vacuumed, however, which is difficult for a small child and often too much trouble for an older one.

• Buy a plastic mat—the type used under office chairs—when a firmer surface than carpet is needed for play.

• Use the best of both. Carpet the bed/dressing area for warm tootsies, and lay vinyl or wood in the play area. Divide them in a pleasing two-to-one proportion, one-third carpet and two-thirds vinyl, or vice versa.

REALITY CHECK

• Don't be too controlling about how a room should be kept. Encourage neatness, but don't demand it. It's their space, after all.

• Choose your battles. Kids are confronted with major issues today: drugs, gangs, sex. Keeping the dialogue open is more important in the grand scheme of things than rigidly enforced neatness.

• Have hope. Some of the biggest slobs turn into neatniks when they have their own places, while some of the most browbeaten have been known to rebel and live in pigsties. Someone once said, "The child you can do the least with will often make you the most proud."

Part IV

CLOSETS AND
A CACHE
OF TIPS

Chapter 22

SHAPING UP
THE CLOSET

We treat our closets the way we treat our bodies; we love stuffing them with good things, but we hate the resulting bulges and lumps.

And like too many pounds on the body, a crammed and crumpled closet makes it harder to get movin' in the morning and look as good as we should throughout the day.

So it pays to put it on a diet and shape it up with some up-to-date equipment.

"You can never be too rich, too thin, or have too much closet space."

—WRITER BILL COSBY

CUTTING THE FAT

Wardrobe consultants say we wear only 20 percent of our clothes 80 percent of the time. The rest are either unflattering, uncomfortable, or beyond repair. We can trim down by scrutinizing each item and asking ourselves:

1. Does it peg me in a stage I should have left behind?

2. Is it flattering and comfortable?

3. Am I saving it for when I lose the extra ten pounds I've been carrying around for ten years?

4. Is that stain or hole going to magically disappear?

5. Do these shoes look as if they've been around the block once too often?

6. Has this underwear seen better days?

7. Has this sleepwear seen better nights?

8. Do I have too many grungy paint, hair-coloring, and gardening clothes?

9. Are two dozen running shirts necessary to the quality of life?

10. Will the mates to these lonely socks and gloves return in this lifetime?

When purging the closet:

• Don't try to tackle it all in one session. Set the kitchen timer for an hour or two, put on a good tape, and work on one section at a time.

• Make three piles on the bed: "charity," "toss," and "alter." Bag and ferry the first, chuck the second, and be realistic about the third. I've found if I'm not motivated to alter or mend an item within a month, I don't really want or need it.

• Reward yourself when the job's done with closet sachet, an organizing accessory, or a great new outfit.

Keeping It Trim

• Cast a wary eye on sales. We sometimes buy things because they seem like bargains, not because they're right for us. Don't buy anything that doesn't make you look and feel sensational.

• Buy year-round clothes. In the limited space of Biosphere 2, a lab that simulated a wide variety of climates for space satellites, male and female scientists packed T-shirts, lightweight wool jumpsuits, cotton sweaters, and jeans for their two-year stay. Year-round clothes can alleviate the space crunch.

• Store out-of-season and formal clothes somewhere other than the bedroom closet.

• Hang space-hungry coats and jackets in the hall closet or on hooks by the back door.

• Keep boots and athletic shoes in the garage or by

the back door to gain space and to avoid making tracks through the house.

- Make sure clothes are clean before they're stored; moths are drawn to perspiration and food stains.

STORE AND ORDER

- Wool needs to breathe. Allow at least an inch between hanging garments, and avoid stacking too many wool sweaters together.
- Don't store clothes in plastic garment bags or airtight plastic boxes. Plastic keeps fabrics from breathing and can discolor and rot them. Fur and leather are particularly susceptible.
- Label storage boxes and trunks with their contents so it's easy to find things when you need them.
- Mothballs are the most effective moth repellent, according to the USDA, but they're toxic to humans, smell bad, and can stain clothes. Keep them out of reach of tiny hands, don't let them touch fabrics, and neutralize the odor with herbs or potpourri. Or better yet, use cedar.
- Line a storage closet, trunk, or drawer with cedar panels, or toss in a few cedar blocks.
- Reactivate cedar's fragrance by sanding boards and blocks every year or two.

OUTFITTING THE SPACE

A closet can be made more functional by rearranging existing rods and adding a few bells and whistles. Surgery isn't necessary, since there's a wide range of space-saving, put-'em-where-you-want-'em, move-'em-to-the-next-place systems at home centers, hardware stores, and closet shops.

You can also call in a closet designer, but a stranger scrutinizing the dark recesses of the closet is more than a lot of us can handle.

- Consider using a vinyl-covered heavy-gauge wire

"True elegance consists not in having a closet bursting with clothes, but rather in having a few well–chosen numbers in which one feels totally at ease."

—COCO CHANEL

THE SMART CLOSET

Closet design has come a long way in the past decade, but for the low-maintenance home, it still has a long way to go. For true convenience, every closet should have:
- *A computer that registers the weather and the day's activities and delivers a fully accessorized outfit right down to the jewelry and shoes.*
- *A carlike warning system that instead of cajoling us to fasten our seat belts, alerts us to lurking stains, unraveling hems, and loose buttons.*
- *A built-in steamer that automatically senses and smooths out wrinkles.*
- *A magnetic system that sucks tossed-on-the-floor shoes into their designated slots.*
- *A three-way mirror slightly distorted to make us look five pounds thinner and five years younger.*

"I did not have 3,000 pairs of shoes. I had 1,060."

—IMELDA MARCOS

system. It offers high visibility, promotes air circulation, and doesn't collect dust.
- Seal existing wood shelves with polyurethane to make them easier to keep clean.
- Move the bedroom bureau into the closet if there's room, or eliminate it altogether by installing pull-out baskets and bins.
- Don't install shelves deeper than twelve inches or items will get pushed back and lost.
- Leave at least a couple of inches between rods and upper shelves for easy hanger removal.
- Store a small, lightweight folding stool for too-tall shelves and too-short you.
- Reclaim space from a deep closet by moving rods closer to the back wall—twelve inches is about right.
- If there's no electrical outlet, mount a battery-operated light on the wall or ceiling.
- Cruise closet shops for organizing accessories: belt hoops, slide-out tie racks, sweater bags, and other innovative space savers.

• Line a small, shallow drawer with velvet for a built-in jewelry box.

• Continue the floor covering into the closet so care is a one-step process.

• Brighten a cavelike interior with glossy white latex walls, or hang a vinyl wall covering in a black-and-white abstract print to camouflage hanger marks.

• Hang a framed poster, photograph, or print as an inspiration for order.

• If a closet is hopelessly small, consider an additional free-standing unit in the bedroom.

"They should put expiration dates on clothes, so we would know when they go out of style."
—GARY SHANDLING

REARRANGING

• Locate all short garments on one side of the closet, long dresses and jumpsuits on another, and leave room for shoe, purse, and sweater shelves somewhere in between.

• Hang short garments double-decker, and if you and the ceiling are high enough, on triple-decker rods.

• Make the most of a tall ceiling by storing occasionally worn items up high.

• Get more mileage out of less space by hanging skirts and pants on multitiered hangers.

• Avoid tangles and creases by replacing wire with plastic, wood, and padded hangers.

• Maintain order by always pointing hanger hooks toward the wall.

• Place shoe, shirt, or gift boxes in drawers to organize socks, stockings, and underwear.

• Get shoes off a dusty floor and into a shoe bag, a rack, or shelves.

PUTTING THE BACK OF THE DOOR TO WORK

• Install tubular towel bars for trousers, ties, shawls, and scarfs.

• Drape chains and long necklaces over adhesive hooks to keep them tangle free.

• Hang a large expandable wooden peg rack for belts, purses, and other accessories.

• Install a few strong hooks to hang the next day's fully accessorized outfit, items needing dry cleaning or repair, and to air a just-worn garment.

DRESSING IN A FLASH

It's 7:00 A.M. Do you know where your outfit is? Mornings can run a lot smoother when we can quickly put our hands on exactly what we need.

• Organize a closet by color as well as category, so everything is easy to locate.

• Put together a week's worth of accessorized outfits, placing jewelry in plastic sandwich bags poked through the hanger.

• Stock up on dresses, so there are fewer separates to coordinate.

• Buy slip-on sweaters with banded bottoms. They don't need to be tucked in, buttoned, or fussed with.

• Pre-tie and pin a scarf over a hanging sweater or dress.

• Keep jewelry to a minimum. One or two statement pieces are more tasteful and easier to don than a lot of bangles and beads.

• Buy neutral-colored, go-with-everything shoes, hose, and bag.

• Have your coloring analyzed by a professional color consultant. Seasonal color schemes coordinate well and steer us to the most flattering wardrobe choices.

• Stick to solid colors. They're easier to mix and match than prints.

• Pack a tote bag the night before with everything that needs to go out the door in the morning.

TROUBLESHOOTING

• Hang or toss things in the laundry basket as they come off. Setting them down to deal with later adds clutter and doubles the work.

• Have a home for everything. It ends frustrating hunts for missing items.

• Check pantyhose for runs as you remove them and everything else for spots, falling hems, and loose threads.

• Don't hang or shelve anything that needs attention.

• If you save only-for-under-slacks pantyhose, keep them in their own box, bin, or bag, separate from the good stuff.

• Hang just-worn but not-quite-ready-for-the-wash clothes inside out to alert you to potential stains and odor.

Chapter 23

MORE TIPS MAMA
NEVER TOLD YOU

"To be happy at home is the ultimate result of all ambition."

—SAMUEL JOHNSON

GRAND ILLUSION

• Keep one room always presentable as a place to escape the mess, and to bamboozle visitors.

• Divert the eye from dusty furnishings, streaked windows, and other offenses with an eye-grabbing focal point: a giant spotlit painting or poster, a striking sculpture, or a big, beautiful arrangement of flowers.

• Use dimmers in every room. Everything, including the occupants, look better in a diffused glow.

• Spray around a little diluted chlorine bleach on the bath and kitchen counters. The odor of disinfectant will make everything seem clean.

FURNISHINGS AND ACCESSORIES

• When refinishing a piece of furniture, sponge a little metallic paint onto the final color coat. The subtle gold, copper, or silver glint will help disguise dust and surface scratches.

• Hide scratches on a conventionally finished piece with a crayon that matches the stain. Crayola makes scores of tones and shades to choose from.

• Manicure nails only on a surface like tile, plastic laminate, or Corian, which can take nail color and polish remover spills.

CLEANING WITHOUT CLEANSERS

It takes time and energy to drag out the cleaning equipment, so here are some quick little fixes that can make a big difference:
- *Put things back.*
- *Toss out old magazines, newspapers, and catalogs.*
- *Bag mail.*
- *Close cabinets, drawers, and doors.*
- *Straighten pictures and lamp shades.*
- *Line up chairs and window coverings.*
- *Plump pillows and cushions.*
- *Fold or artfully toss throw blankets.*
- *Unwrap a new bar of "fresh" scented soap for the bathroom (Irish Spring works well).*
- *Throw a tablecloth over a dusty table.*
- *Chuck dead plants and flowers.*
- *Change the cat litter.*
- *Train the dog to sit and stay on the carpet stain.*
- *Send the kids next door.*
- *Turn down the lights.*
- *Pour yourself a cold one.*
- *Close your eyes and visualize a clean home.*

- Glue felt pads on the bottoms of vases, table lamps, and other accessories to prevent table scratches.
- Fill vases with glass florist pebbles to give them stability and for easy flower arranging.
- Add a dose of cut flower food to the water. It inhibits algae and prolongs the life of flowers.
- Buy opaque vases so you don't see the water cloud as stems break down.
- Avoid silk, dried, and plastic flowers. They collect dust and look ratty over time. The beauty of real flowers may be fleeting, but that's part of their charm.
- Prevent plaster crumbles and drywall dust when hanging a picture by placing a cross of tape over the spot where the nail is to be pounded.

• Choose a telephone in a simple, sleek design that won't attract grime and a dark color to hide fingerprints.

STORAGE

• Provide plenty of closed storage. Actress Jacqueline Bisset was quoted in *Woman's Day* as saying she grew up battling disorder because she and her family lived in a 300-year-old house that didn't have one built-in cupboard.

• Make a side table with a secret. Have the lumber store cut a thirty-inch round of plywood to top a forty-gallon trash can. Drape it to the floor with an approximately sixty-inch round tablecloth and a thirty-inch round of glass. Store out-of-season clothing, holiday decorations, extra bedding, or whatever, inside.

• Store travel cosmetics, toiletries, compact umbrella, battery-operated reading light, and other trip necessities in your most-used suitcase.

• Buy a label maker (under ten dollars at office suppliers) to neatly label everything from children's dresser drawers to storage boxes.

• Allocate one shelf in the house for library books, so they don't disappear into your own collection.

• Round up phone books in a big wicker basket.

• Paint a line around the outside of a paint can to indicate the paint level and color.

BABYPROOFING

Instead of making it into the "House of No-No," for their safety and your sanity it's crucial to:

• Cap all electrical outlets.
• Hang stair gates.
• Store all medicines, cleaning supplies, and sharp tools out of reach.
• Put away breakables.
• Replace table and floor lamps with wall and ceiling lights.

- Round all sharp corners.
- Replace glass tabletops.
- Place houseplants out of reach.
- Use materials that will get you through the formula-and-creamed-spinach and into the peanut-butter-and-jelly stage.

"Discipline becomes a habit that frees you to plan your time."
—ALEXANDRA STODDARD

CHILDPROOFING

- Consider converting a section of the basement, attic, or even the garage into a rainy-day playroom.
- Move the TV out of a room you want to stay neater, since it's such a magnet for messes.
- Place a dishpan or bucket filled with soapy water by the back door so kids can wash up before they come in from the sandbox or mud pile.
- Rig up an outdoor shower in the summer, when kids get especially grungy from play.
- Place a shoe rack inside the back door and train kids to kick off footwear *before* they make tracks.
- Store outdoor toys in a large lidded trash can so they'll stay clean, dry, and easy to find.
- Confine paints, crayons, and markers to one designated area, so there's no temptation to play Van Gogh in the living room.
- Spread a plastic drop cloth on the floor for finger painting, egg dyeing, and other wet and messy projects.
- Use a newspaper or magazine as a base for pasting. Just turn the page for a new clean surface.
- Keep a supply of paper cups on hand. Write the child's name on it and challenge her to see how long she can make it last.
- Keep water-filled plastic sports bottles in the fridge for self-service. Water is the best thirst quencher and won't stain fabrics, furnishings, and floors.
- Protect the sofa and upholstered chairs with canvas drop cloths that the kids have hand-painted (on a stain-proof floor) themselves.

• Hang art with heavy-duty hardware that can withstand roughhousing.
• Toss out-of-place toys and clothing in a "doghouse" basket. Assign an extra chore to retrieve it.

To Market to Market

• Be loyal to one grocery store. Knowing the layout and the merchandise saves time and trouble.
• Keep a running grocery list by the fridge, so items get noted as they run out.
• Use hieroglyphics on the list for faster shopping: √: produce, 0: dairy, *: toiletries and medicines, ~: frozen.
• Consolidate errands like banking, shoe repair, and dry cleaning on the way to or from the store.
• Keep a plastic beach basket in the backseat of the car to keep small packages together and to haul them easily into the house.
• Keep a carton in the car trunk to contain bags of groceries, take-out foods, potluck meals, bake-sale contributions, flower arrangements, and such.

The Garage

• Keep a wastebasket on the driver's side of the garage so car debris is easily dumped.
• Lay a big rectangle of cardboard under the car to absorb oil and other drips.
• Paint the floor with a clear concrete sealer to keep dust down.
• Paint parking spaces for bikes, skateboards, wagons, and scooters. Stencil users' names on each space so they'll be motivated to use them.
• Assign a shelf to each family member for shoes and equipment.
• Keep an "everything" box in a corner for mysterious nuts and bolts and other orphaned flotsam and jetsam. Dump it annually.

• Use clear labeled storage containers so you don't have to dump the works each time you need something.

• Ferry trash cans and recycling bins out to the curb on a skateboard or dolly.

• Install plenty of hooks for shovels, rakes, and ladders.

• Outline the silhouettes of tools on pegboard and other walls so they get put back where they belong without thinking.

• Screw a few towel racks into the walls to hold poles, lumber, and other long, toppling items.

• Keep a portable screen near the worktable to contain dust when sanding or sawing.

• Keep your eyes attuned to clutter. Few things have a shorter life than a neat garage.

"I have no doubt that over the years my children will find plenty of things about me to criticize. But something tells me that twenty years from now not one of them will sit on some therapist's couch complaining because their mother didn't spend enough time vacuuming up glitter."

—JOYCE MAYNARD

CHRISTMAS

• If your talents lie in baking and a friend likes to wrap gifts or address cards, have a chore exchange.

• When choosing gifts for others, think twice before buying anything that requires high maintenance.

• Shop early for out-of-state gifts, and have stores wrap and deliver. Some offer this service free as an incentive to shop before Thanksgiving.

• Phone in for advertised specials. The delivery charge is usually less than the price of gas.

• Request the courtesy wrap, which is often a pretty box and a ribbon. Wrapping paper really isn't necessary if the box is festive. Think of all the wrapping and cleanup saved without it.

• Choose a Scotch pine, balsam, or Douglas fir tree for needle retention. Spruces drop needles quickly as they dry out.

• Lay a jumbo trash bag under the tree to protect the floor from spills and to catch falling needles when the tree goes out the door.

• Either have guests contribute side dishes for the

"The pioneers cleared the forests from Jamestown to the Mississippi with fewer tools than are stored in the typical modern garage."

—DWAYNE LAWS

holiday dinner or invite them over early, assign tasks, and enjoy the chaotic camaraderie.

• Have a tree-undressing party, so you don't get stuck with the job. Announce the date ahead of time, pop some corn, lay a fire, and rent a video for afterward.

• Consider forgoing the whole Christmas routine and spending the money on a family vacation.

TIMESAVERS

• Use what Messies Anonymous founder and author Sandra Felton calls "little minutes": making the bed while the coffee brews, wiping the sink while the curling iron heats, straightening a desk while talking on the phone. "Used effectively," said Felton, "little minutes reap hours of relaxation."

• Exercise the dog during your daily walk or run.

• Combine children's bath and story time. While they soak, you tell the tale.

• After dinner, make tomorrow's lunches, lay out clothes, set the breakfast table, ask the kids if they need permission slips signed, field trip money, show-and-tell items, and such. Last-minute surprises are no fun, and studies show it takes 20 percent longer to do things in the morning than in the evening.

• Anticipate. Fill the gas tank before it gets too low. Buy detergent, postage stamps, milk, etc., before you've run out.

• Invest in a speakerphone for the home office, kitchen, and/or other work space, so you can talk and maneuver at the same time.

• Screen dinnertime calls with your answering machine; 6 to 8 P.M. is high time for telemarketers.

• Buy multiples of high-demand, frequently disappearing items: scissors, tape, pens, keys, and notepads.

• Allocate time in the morning to tidying up before you leave. It'll make a difference when you come home tired and cranky.

- Never go from room to room emptyhanded. As a flight attendant, I learned not to walk down an aisle without delivering or retrieving a tray, a drink, or a child.
- Use a big basket to scoop up and deliver out-of-place items.
- Keep the place always looking shipshape and your weekends free by spending five minutes a day tidying up each room. Use a kitchen timer to keep you on track.
- Mom may have told you to hit every surface in a room, but if it ain't dirty, don't clean it.

INDEX